RED MOON OVER SPAIN

CANADIAN MEDIA REACTION
TO·THE
SPANISH CIVIL WAR
1936·1939

MARY·BIGGAR·PECK

Steel Rail

ARMED WORKERS, FARMERS OPPOSE REVOLTING MOROCCANS
. The "Rightist" revolution which started in Spanish Morocco spread to the Montana army barracks at Madrid to-day, the rebels reportedly surrendering after a four-hour bombardment. Virtually in control of all Spanish Morocco, military rebels landed in Spain, and were met by armed volunteers. African forces, according to a government statement, were landed at Algecras "through the treason of the commander of the warship Churruca." The map shows the scene of the strife.

Toronto Star, July 20, 1936. Metropolitan Toronto Library Board photo.

RED MOON OVER SPAIN

CANADIAN MEDIA REACTION

TO·THE

SPANISH CIVIL WAR

1936·1939

Canadian Cataloguing in Publication Data

Peck, Mary Biggar
    Red Moon over Spain : Canadian media reaction to the
Spanish Civil War, 1936-1939

Includes index.
Bibliography: p.
ISBN 0-88791-037-8

    1. Spain--History--Civil War, 1936-1939--Foreign
public opinion, Canadian--Sources. 2. Public
opinion--Canada--History--20th century--Sources.
3. Foreign news--Canada--History--20th century--
Sources. I. Title.

PN4908.P43 1988   946.081   C88-090361-9

Cover Design: David Berman TypoGraphics, Ottawa
Printing: Love Printing Service Inc., Ottawa

This book has been published with the assistance of the Canada Council
and the Ontario Arts Council.

ISBN 0-88791-037-8

Steel Rail Publishing, Ottawa

Table of Contents

Acknowledgements

I began work on this topic 20 years ago at Carleton University. Therefore, my first thanks should go to Professor Tom Middlebro', supervisor of my project, and to the six distinguished Canadians who granted me interviews at that time. Wilfred Kesterton, Eugene Forsey, Frank Scott, Hazen Sise, Graham Spry and Joseph Thorson provided invaluable information on the Spanish Civil War, the CCF and Communist parties, economic conditions, and the media in Canada and abroad during the 1930s. I also appreciate the persistence of my friend, Dr. Eleanor Sutherland, who has constantly urged me to complete and publish the material I assembled in 1968.

During the past six months, many people have helped me. I am grateful for the immediate interest shown by Steel Rail Publishing when I took my original manuscript to them, and for the cooperation of Hounslow Press when I postponed work for them in order to complete *Red Moon Over Spain* for the 50th anniversary of the withdrawal of the International Brigades from Spain.

As usual, the staffs of both the National Archives and the National Library of Canada have been very helpful, especially Sharon Uno of the Photography Section and Jack D'Aoust, Head of the Reprography Unit. Alan Walker of the Toronto Metropolitan Library's Canadian History Department was most efficient in supervising the reproduction of many items from magazines and newspapers. Mr. James Cherrier, Manager of the Toronto Star Syndicate, obtained permission for me to reprint material from the *Toronto Star*. The Archives of the Province of Manitoba, of the City of Edmonton and of Calgary's Glenbow Institute provided photographs, as did Dorothy Livesay, Ted Allan and Yousuf Karsh. Ms. Livesay's kind permission to reprint three of her poems is much appreciated. The Communist Party of Canada permitted me to use several photographs from their collection at the National Archives of Canada.

I am most grateful to Terry Binnersley of Steel Rail Publishing for all her work on the book, including editing, to which Olive Koyama and my daughter Barbara also contributed. As always, my husband George Peck devoted his time and skills whenever and wherever needed, especially in the areas of typing and of map and layout preparation.

Red Moon

And this same pallid moon tonight,
Which rides so quiet – clear and high –
The mirror of our pale and troubled gaze,
Raised to a cool Canadian sky,
Above the shattered Spanish mountain tops
Last night rose low and wild and red,
Reflecting back from her illumined shield
The blood-bespattered faces of the dead.
To that pale moon I raise my angry fist
And to those nameless dead my vows renew:
Comrades who fall in angry loneliness,
Who die for us – I will remember you.

– Norman Bethune, 1936

Introduction

I grew up in Montreal in the 1930s and the Spanish Civil War was the great cause of my youth. Most of the students in my high school were children of European immigrants, and the time when Hazen Sise came to speak to us about his recent experiences in Spain is probably as vivid a memory to them as it still is to me. A young architect and a member of a prominent Montreal family, Sise was just beginning practice in London, England when he met Dr. Norman Bethune, and went to work with him on his blood transfusion unit in Spain. Tall and handsome, dressed in the simple outfit he had worn in Spain, Sise looked to us like Galahad in shining armour.

Today it is difficult for revisionist historians to comprehend what Philip Toynbee described as "the whole marvellous atmosphere of conspiracy and purpose"[1] that existed in the 1930s, when the young joined together to fight against poverty, capitalism, Fascism and war. But while many prominent British statesmen and intellectuals supported the Spanish Loyalists, this did not happen in Canada. Few influential Canadians were interested in the cause of the Spanish government, which was supported by the working class and the Communist and CCF parties. Memories of the Spanish Civil War quickly dimmed after World War Two broke out, only a few months after the struggle ended in Spain.

During the anti-Communist paranoia of the 1950s, many of the Canadians who had fought in Spain had trouble finding jobs. I once heard Norman Bethune's niece describe in a television interview how her family had destroyed all her uncle's memorabilia at the time of the McCarthy trials in the United States.

When I was attending graduate school in Canadian Studies at Carleton University in 1967, the subject of Canadian public opinion on the Spanish Civil War appeared on a list of essay topics. I was amazed to find that I was the only student interested in the subject! In fact, the Civil War and Bethune had been almost forgotten, and Franco still ruled Spain. The following year I expanded the essay I had written into a major research paper. This book is a revised version of that paper.

In 1971, Canada recognized the government of what was then called Red China, an event which forced Canadians to acknowledge Bethune's existence and his fame in China. When the first Chinese delegates arrived in Canada, they immediately asked to be shown the monuments and buildings "dedicated to our beloved Dr. Bethune." This must have embarrassed Canadian diplomats, as at the time there was not even a historic plaque on Bethune's birthplace in Gravenhurst, Ontario.

But the Spanish Civil War did influence a number of writers and filmmakers over the past 30 years. Rick in *Casablanca* lost his idealism while running guns for the Republic; in *La Guerre est Finie,* directed by Alain Resnais, Yves Montand played the role of a Spanish political exile, a man trapped between his past as an ardent supporter of Spanish freedom and his future of almost certain imprisonment if he returned to his country as a secret agent. The war appears as a symbol of a generation's attitude in the works of British playwright Arnold Wesker and in the novels of Montreal's Mordecai Richler – in fact, it is a recurring theme in the mind of Richler's anti-hero in *Joshua Then and Now.* A biography of Bethune by Ted Allan and Sydney Gordon, *The Scalpel, the Sword,* was published in 1952. The National Film Board made a documentary on the Mackenzie-Papineau Battalion, the Canadians who fought in Spain. And the CBC has produced a television drama starring Donald Sutherland as Bethune, as well as a two-part programme on the Spanish Civil War. More recently, *Gone the Burning Sun,* Ken Mitchell's play on the life of Bethune, has been performed in Canada and China. But in all this time, no one has written about the varied opinions on the Spanish Civil War that appeared in Canadian publications from 1936 to 1939.

In October 1986, when a rebel supply plane carrying several Americans was shot down in Nicaragua, President Reagan compared the Contra forces to the Abraham Lincoln Battalion that fought in Spain. Americans were free to aid the rebel Contras, he announced, adding, "Some years ago many of you spoke of something called the American Lincoln Brigade [*sic*] in the Spanish Civil War." The comparison infuriated the 100 American veterans of the Abraham Lincoln Battalion who were revisiting the battlefields of Spain on the 50th anniversary of the beginning of the war. "We were fighting against fascism and for freedom," said 84-year-old Steve Nelson, commissar of the battalion. "What are the Contras fighting for?"[2]

About two years ago, I saw a very moving account of the American volunteers in a feature-length documentary entitled *The Good Fight.* As proof of its wide appeal, the film was playing at a theatre near my home in Ottawa; I later read a laudatory review in the *Daily Telegraph,* written while the film was playing at the Rio Theatre in London, England. In the film, eleven veterans of the campaign – soldiers, nurses and a woman ambulance driver – tell their stories, interspersed with archival material. It is clear that they were well aware of the war's romantic appeal, but they are uncompromising about why they went: they were committed to stopping the march of Fascism in Europe. At the film's end, a small group of the veterans is shown participating in a protest march. A rag-tag and undisciplined crew, waving placards as they swing along, they are in striking contrast to the World War Two veterans who march in step each year on November 11th, maintaining a military bearing as they formally approach the War Memorial.

The 50th anniversary of the withdrawal of the International Brigades from the Spanish Civil War has renewed interest in these previously unsung heroes. The hundred-odd surviving Canadian veterans have given up their long fight for veterans' pensions, but they still seek official recognition of the important role they played prior to World War Two. On February 1, 1988, an editorial in the *Ottawa Citizen* discussed a brief report issued by the Commons Veterans Affairs Committee. The editorial stated that the parliamentary committee is finally

ready to make peace with the then-young Canadians who fought in the Spanish Civil War with the Mackenzie-Papineau Battalion. Denounced as Communists at the time – some were; some were only young – the Mac-Paps inspired an official disapproval in the mid-1930s that persists today in some corners of the Tory caucus.[3]

The report says of the Mac-Paps, "They acted out of conscience, and this merits respect whether one agrees with what they did or not."

It is sad that the committee offered such a grudging acknowledgement of the battalion's cause, a cause since proven to have been a just one. But the committee's attitude is not surprising given Canadian government policy during the war. Despite Canada's official non-interventionist stance, supplies shipped from Canada were reaching Franco's forces through Morocco at the same time that Canadians were officially forbidden to fight on behalf of the Loyalist government.

Red Moon Over Spain is intended to clarify an aspect of Canadian history that has long been neglected. Today few Canadians know the reaction at home to the role played by the Canadian volunteers who fought in the Spanish Civil War. I hope that the veterans of the Mackenzie-Papineau Battalion, members of their families and all those interested in the chaotic period of the 1930s will enjoy this study of the prejudices, political beliefs, hopes and fears expressed by Canadians during the Spanish Civil War.

Ottawa, 1988

CHAPTER 1

"The Darkling Plain"

And we are here as on a darkling plain
Swept with confused alarms of struggle and flight,
Where ignorant armies clash by night.
   – "Dover Beach," Matthew Arnold

It is now nine years that men of my generation have had
Spain within their hearts, nine years that they have carried it
with them like an evil wound. It was in Spain that men
learned that one can be right and yet be beaten, that force can
vanquish spirit, that there are times when courage is not its
own recompense. It is this, doubtless, which explains why so
many men the world over, feel the Spanish drama as a
personal tragedy.

   – Albert Camus[1]

It is now 50 years since the International Brigades withdrew from Spain near the end of the Spanish Civil War, but the intense feelings of engagement and bitterness described by Camus persist. This complex war has been called "the last Crusade" and "the last Great Cause." In 1961, Hugh Thomas' *The Spanish Civil War* was on the best-seller list for months, and in 1968 André Malraux mentioned "the only important thing thirty years ago, the Spanish Civil War."[2] The 1930s were a time of social upheaval, and the literary commitment to politics reflected the decade's concerns. Vincent Brome felt that "the guilt of a privileged upbringing converted many an academic to a brand of Marxism which regarded the proletariat as the chosen people."[3]

The struggle in Spain aroused international passions and polarized public opinion. *Red Moon Over Spain* attempts to trace, through the written media, Canadian reactions to the conflict. Newspapers and periodicals representing varied points of view have been researched. The newspapers were restricted to four important periods of the war: the opening of hostilities, the Battle of Madrid, the attack on Guernica, and the end of the war. The periodicals were examined for its duration; this was usually necessary to obtain enough material to be of value.

II

When the Spanish Church declined in the twentieth century, the chief unifying force in the country lost its vitality. By 1930, it is estimated that only one-third of Spaniards were practising Roman Catholics. The church hierarchy was commonly regarded as the ally of the upper classes, whose stranglehold on agriculture was the main sore point throughout the country. Landlords hired daily labourers living in dreary villages for low wages, and often did not bother to work their land at all. Tenant farmers were little better off than labourers, as they held small plots of land on short leases.

When the Republic replaced the Monarchy without bloodshed in 1931, Spaniards expected a brave new world. Instead, the new constitution of that year, with its anti-clerical and agricultural reforms and its support for the independent Catalans and Basques, resulted in the alignment of Spain along two fronts; liberals and the working class supported local rights while the Church, wealthy landowners

"(5) A street scene in the heart of Madrid. The street is the Calle de Alcela. The bank of Spain is on the right, and in the centre is the ministry of communications." *Toronto Star*, August 25, 1936. Metropolitan Toronto Library Board photo.

---

and army favoured central control. A self-indulgent ruling class strongly opposed the democratic government so fervently desired by workers and the lower middle class.

The years between 1933 and 1935 were known as *Bienio Negro,* black years of battles between the Communists and the Fascists. A revolt led by the miners in the province of Asturias was brutally crushed by the army, directed from Madrid by the Chief of Staff, General Francisco Franco. Young army officers formed the UME, a group dedicated to the overthrow of the Republic, which was also the aim of the fascist Falange and the Monarchists.

It soon became apparent that the Second Republic was endangered not only by its opponents on the right but also by the differences in beliefs and methods of its left-wing, comprising Anarcho-Syndicalists (CNT), Anarchists (FAI), Trotskyists (POUM) and Socialists (UGT).

Inspired by the idea of a popular front against Fascism proposed by the Communist International in 1935, all the Spanish left groups joined together. In the February election of 1936, the Popular Front won a majority of the seats in the Cortes, or Spanish parliament. However, the centre and right together had a small majority of the votes cast.

From the time of the election, violence, murder and arson spread across the country, caused in part by the release from jail of all political prisoners, and by the efforts of the Falange to spread disorder. By the end of June, the army chiefs and the Monarchists were prepared to start an uprising. On July 11th, a British plane, chartered by a Monarchist newspaperman, transported Franco from the Canaries, where he was in semi-exile, to Spanish Morocco, where he would soon seize command of the Army

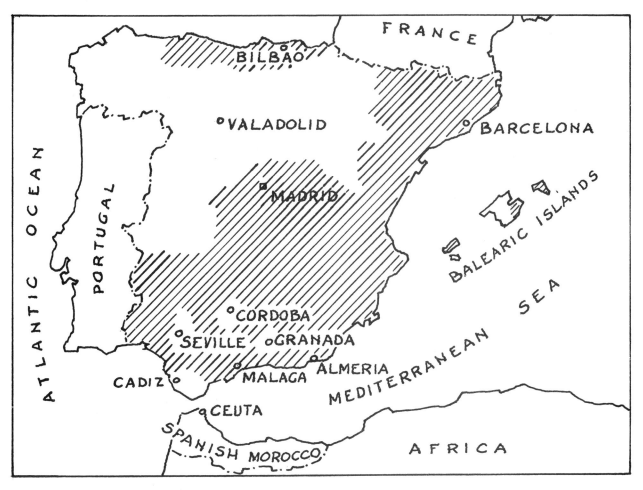

LOYALIST ZONE
NATIONALIST ZONE

Map of Spain, divided into Republican and Nationalist zones, July 1936. Drawn by G.W. Peck.

of Africa. On July 12th, an officer in the *Asaltos,* or special constabulary, was the second in his force to be shot to death within a month. The following day, several of the *Asaltos* shot and killed Jose Calvo Sotelo, head of the Monarchist party. These events and rumours of a Communist plot to overthrow the Republic gave the Falange and generals the opportunity they had been waiting for. Finally, on the night of July 17-18th, the generals called out the garrisons in northern Morocco and the war began.

The garrison in each town established a standard pattern of revolt by attempting to seize the Town Hall, radio system, Post Office, and other strong points. This would leave only the trade unions and left-wing parties to support the government. The Rebel troops or "Nationalists" were very strong, consisting of the Army of Africa containing the Foreign Legion and Moorish troops, the Civil Guard and two-thirds of the army in Spain. The Republic,

whose defenders were called "Loyalists," was very short of arms and trained men, but did control the industrial regions and the Bank of Spain with its huge gold reserves.

Although Church and State were closely linked in Nationalist Spain, where the enemies of the state were freemasons, union leaders and Popular Front supporters, it did not seem incongruous to the Nationalists that the Moors were allies and the Roman Catholic Basques enemies. On the other side, the anti-clerical Loyalists accepted the strongly Catholic Basques as allies. Republican Spain attacked the churches as the outposts of middle- or upper-class morality and manners. Journalist Pierre van Paassen once described a religious procession in Seville where priests, wearing vestments of gold and carrying a statue of the virgin literally buried under jewels, were followed by hollow-cheeked, barefoot and ragged women and children. Accord-

"(1) The Holy Family Church in Barcelona, where vestments and pews were removed and burned in the streets, according to a letter received by Elsie McLaughlin of Toronto. (2) Loyalists firing from a church belfry during a street battle." *Toronto Star*, August 25, 1936. Metropolitan Toronto Library Board photo.

ing to Hugh Thomas, nearly 8,000 clerics were killed, and "at no time in the history of Europe has so passionate a hatred of religion and all its works been shown."[4] While the fiercely anti-clerical bias of the Loyalists was a revenge upon the institution that had betrayed them, the campaign against the Church made Loyalist Spain unpopular in many countries.

Both sides appealed to European governments for help and the question of aid became part of the power politics preceding World War Two. Germany and Italy seized the chance to show strength, weaken France, and try out weapons, planes and troops. The Soviet Union soon began to contribute equipment to the Republican forces and to organize the International Brigades of volunteer soldiers from around the world to aid the Popular Front and further the anti-Fascist cause. This intervention by the Soviet Union was used as an excuse not to provide aid to the elected government and later to discredit the survivors of the international forces when they returned from Spain.

Premier Léon Blum, head of the Popular Front government in France, pledged support to the Republic but gave in to pressure from Great Britain and, except for brief periods, the border between

Spain and France remained closed. The refusal of the Conservative government in Britain to aid the Loyalists was couched in diplomatic terms but was in fact tacit support for the Rebels. During the diplomatic battle of August 1936, a non-intervention plan was accepted in principle by France, Britain, Italy and Russia, as well as by smaller European powers. At the same time that Anthony Eden started to arrange a non-intervention committee, Italy and Russia began to aid the side that they supported in Spain. Delegates from many European countries including Germany attended the committee's first meeting in London in September 1936. Thus was born what the German ambassador to Britain, von Ribbentrop, sarcastically called "the Intervention Committee,"[5] which was to graduate from equivocation to hypocrisy and last out the Civil War.

Hugh Thomas believes that the war would certainly have taken a different course if the Republic had been able to purchase arms from Britain, the United States and France, and that, while the non-intervention policy was reasonable at first, it was cynical of Britain to insist on its maintenance. Such cynicism was of no advantage, as a general war fought over Spain would have been more favourable for Great Britain than the one fought in 1939.

While their governments sought to avoid the significance of the Fascist powers' presence in Spain, some citizens made positive attempts to prevent the war from spreading. In the first week of September 1936, 5,000 representatives from 32 nations met in Brussels to attend the Universal Peace Conference. Members of trade unions, women's organizations, youth groups and veterans' associations hoped to create a coordinating bureau and permanent congress for peace. However, speeches by dignitaries and resolutions from 20 committees were in vain without official support from the Great Powers.

Twenty Canadians attended as delegates, among them Tim Buck, National Secretary of the Communist Party of Canada, and Allan Dowd, also a Communist and a social worker. They went on to Spain and Dowd remained very involved throughout the war. He made arrangements for delegates of the Spanish government to visit Canada and the United States the following month, arbitrated Dr. Norman Bethune's difficulties with his Spanish colleagues in 1937, and negotiated the repatriation of the Canadian volunteers in 1939.[6]

At the beginning of the war, the Loyalists occupied all the south and east of Spain as well as the northern Basque provinces. The opening of hostilities was accompanied by a social revolution in many Loyalist areas. The interest of the world was aroused during the Battle of Madrid in November and December 1936, when the civilian population rose to defend the city, street by street, and building by building. This was followed by the war in the north – the attack on Guernica, the epic of Bilbao and the Basques, and the battles of Brunete and Belchite. The war of attrition from December 1937 to November 1938 saw a slow, inexorable decline for the Loyalists marked by the battles of Teruel and the Ebro and the Aragon offensive.

Canadian volunteers went to Spain early in the war and they first saw action at Jarama River with the Abraham Lincoln Battalion from February to April 1937. Some Canadians fought with the Washington Battalion at Brunete in July. The Mackenzie-Papineau Battalion composed of Canadian and American volunteers had been formed in June as part of the XVth International Brigade. The battalion went into action at Fuentes de Ebro in October, fighting until the withdrawal of the International Brigades in September 1938. Not until 1939 was the final blow struck, with the fall of Barcelona in January, followed by recognition of Franco's Nationalist government by France and Great Britain in March.

III

More than 1,200 men went from Canada to fight in Spain for the Loyalist government. What was the background of those who volunteered to fight for Spain?

In Canada, this decade, known as "the Dirty Thirties," was a time of poverty and despair for many people. Following the stock market crash of 1929, the United States imposed higher tariffs on Canadian goods which, along with cost-cutting efforts, helped throw many people out of work. Unemployment insurance did not exist and relief for the poor was deliberately ungenerous. By the winter of 1933, an estimated 32 percent of Canadian wage-earners were out of work. Added to these economic problems was the ecological disaster on the Prairies, where people saw their farmland dry up and blow away before their eyes.

Single young men, unwilling to be a burden on

Unemployed No. 5.   *From a lithograph by Ernst Neumann*

New Frontier, April 1936, Metropolitan Toronto Library Board photo.

Seated in front of a portrait of herself, a Toronto debutante prepares 500 invitations to a dinner dance held to celebrate her formal entrance into Toronto society. *Toronto Star*, November 19, 1936. Metropolitan Toronto Library Board photo.

A protester being evicted from the Vancouver Post Office in 1937. National Archives of Canada/ C-79026.

their families, and unable to get relief if they chose to seek work elsewhere, often became transients, living in hobo jungles. By 1932, the government established work camps, where the men received food, clothing and 20 cents a day. The men felt that much of the work they did was useless, their lives dull and futureless.

During this time the chief organization to provide a channel for the futility felt by the unemployed men was the Communist Party. It organized the Relief Camp Workers Union and led the On-to-Ottawa Trek, which culminated in the Dominion Day Riot in Regina and the occupation of the Central Post Office in Vancouver. In spite of all efforts, the Conservative government of R.B. Bennett remained unmoved and, as predicted by economist Leonard Marsh in the 1930s, the drift of some Canadians into a cycle of chronic dependence was one of the Depression's tragic legacies.

Similarly, the Communist Party was an active force in the trade union movement, while the mainstream labour organizations were losing members and failing to organize new industrial workers, and the government did very little to combat the worst effects of the Depression.

It was these men, who saw the lack of democracy in action at home and feared the rise of Fascism in Europe, who went to fight in the International Brigades in Spain. Meanwhile, the powers-that-be were horrified by the rise of the "Communist menace" in Canada and were determined not to aid its cause in Spain.

Victor Hoar has told the story of the Canadians who fought in Spain in his book *The Mackenzie-Papineau Battalion,* but no one has written about the attitudes of other Canadians towards the Spanish Civil War. This book attempts to show the extent of the interest and involvement in the war in Canada, as well as the strong opposition to Canadian support for the Loyalist side.

The legacy of the Spanish Civil War was often a bitter one, and news coverage reflected the divided feelings and attitudes of the event itself. In Spain, each side issued news reports, usually irreconcilable, so newspapers in Canada could choose, according to their prejudices, what they wished to portray. The *New York Times* even sent reporters to present both sides of the struggle, the pro-Loyalist Herbert Matthews and the pro-Rebel William Carney. Censorship added to the bewilderment of the reader and favoured the Rebels, who restricted reporters greatly, while the Loyalists welcomed everyone, including Major Clement Atlee, later Labour Prime Minister of Great Britain, Ernest Hemingway and Paul Robeson.

It is easy to be wise long after events have occurred, and journalists and editors of the period had no access to an objective analysis like that done by Hugh Thomas. I have used his book to a large extent for the historical background and events of the war. Allen Guttmann's work on American opinion concerning the war in *The Wound in the Heart* was of use in comparing Canadian and American attitudes.

Information from newspapers tends to be voluminous and often polemical. In order to counteract this, an effort was made to use all sections of the paper: headlines, editorials, columns, cartoons and letters to the editor, often very indicative of current issues. Professor Peter Waite once spoke of newspapers as being always "à parti pris," and in 1936 Professor Eugene Forsey said that fighting the Montreal *Gazette* or *Star* by means of letters was "like fighting a feather bed."[7] However, to some extent, letters to the editor may express a definite change in public opinion, while allowing a variety of viewpoints in newspapers whose policy and readers are dissimilar.

If the resistance of the Spanish people became in many ways a focus for the democratic struggles and the progressive movement in the Thirties, it also gave courage to the writers and poets pushing to extend the boundaries of art and culture beyond the upper and middle classes. The Spanish Civil War seemed a last hope, a last opportunity to do something in the face of a world gone mad.

CHAPTER 2

"The Church's one foundation is now the Moslem sword"

The Church's one foundation
Is now the Moslem sword,
In meek collaboration
With flame and axe and cord;
Deep-winged with holy love
The battle-planes of Wotan,
The bombing-place of Jove.
     – Louis A. MacKay[1]

The Canadian publications I examined fall into two categories: those which were anti-Loyalist and supported Franco, though to varying degrees, and those which were pro-Loyalist, always without equivocation. In the first category were five newspapers and two periodicals: *La Patrie, Le Devoir* and the *Gazette*, all of Montreal; the *Globe and Mail*, *Maclean's* and *Saturday Night*, all of Toronto; and *Le Droit* of Ottawa. Pro-Loyalist publications included the *Toronto Star, Winnipeg Free Press, Vancouver Province*, the *Federationist* of British Columbia, and the *New Commonwealth, Canadian Forum* and *New Frontier*, all of Toronto. This chapter deals with anti-Loyalist newspapers, while pro-Loyalist newspapers are reviewed in Chapter 3. Chapter 4 compares the periodicals pro and con.

McKim's Directory of Canadian Publications[2] gave the circulation of the *Globe* in September 1936 as 78,395. The *Globe* was listed as Independent Liberal and the *Mail and Empire*, with which it united in October 1936, as Independent Conservative. The circula-tion of the *Mail* at that time was 118,389 and *McKim's* characterized the *Mail and Empire* audience "an 'able to buy' audience."

While Liberal in politics, the *Globe* was a conservative paper compared to others in Toronto. It did not become Conservative in policy until some time after George McCullagh became publisher in 1936. On November 23rd of that year, *Saturday Night* accused the *Globe and Mail* of trying to appeal to the tabloid mentality by changing its middle-class, Liberal orientation.

In Montreal, the *Gazette*, Independent Conservative, with a circulation of 30,171, emphasized "the wealthy market reached by the *Gazette*." The Montreal *Daily Star*, listed as Independent with a circulation of 118,996, "Concentrates on the Inner Circle, English-speaking Montreal." Both had a middle-class commercial orientation with relatively little difference in policy. The *Gazette* editorials were rather pallid and, under Lord Atholstan, the *Daily Star* was conservative in tone, compared to the more forceful Toronto papers of the period.

Among French-language papers, *La Presse* had the largest circulation, 150,168. In an interview in April 1969, Wilfred Kesterton, head of Carleton University's School of Journalism, termed it an omnibus type of paper at this time, after an earlier lurid period. He felt that *La Patrie*, "Canada's Dynamic French newspaper," was much more likely to be interested in the Civil War than *La Presse*.

Listed as Independent, its weekday circulation was 14,856, but on Sundays it soared to 78,778. Its attitude to the Spanish Civil War was quite similar to that of *Le Devoir*.

Started by Henri Bourassa as Liberal, but Bleu, in this period *Le Devoir* had a strong Roman Catholic orientation under Omer Heroux, who signed most of the editorials. Listed as Independent with a circulation of 22,251, it described itself as "A French Daily of Quality for Quality people, the national roadway leading directly to the élite of French Canada." *Le Devoir* appealed to the French Canadian intelligentsia and *La Patrie* to a less educated readership. Both, however, supported the views of the Roman Catholic Church and their attitudes to the Spanish Civil War did not differ greatly, except that *Le Devoir* was at times more rational and less sensational in its approach. The French-language papers represented the thinking of the Church, which at that time was solidly behind the state and big business complex in Quebec.

Maclean's magazine, described as "general and national" with a circulation of 254,229, as compared to *Liberty's* 215,473, was part of Colonel Maclean's magazine-publishing empire. *Saturday Night* with a circulation of 1,500, approximately the same number as the *Canadian Forum*, described itself as literary and non-partisan, intended for the professional and businessman. This brief look at the history and background of the anti-Loyalist publications helps to explain their conservative outlook.

Until after World War Two, the Canadian Press, a national newspaper cooperative, had few correspondents outside the country. For that reason it relied greatly upon Associated Press, an American newsgathering agency with a reputation for accuracy and impartiality. The chief complaint of Canadian papers and readers was that A.P. foreign news was selected for American readers and the same news passed on to Canada. It was felt that insufficient British news was supplied and, by 1936, C.P. was obtaining news reports from Reuters, a British agency, and Havas, a French one.

Both Charles Havas and Julius Reuter started their agencies by specializing in financial news. The inference has been drawn that both the armaments industry and the government in France were in a position to influence the kind of news distributed by Havas. Léon Blum quarrelled with Mr. Havas in 1936 concerning this control. Reuters was regarded as the news agency of the British Empire, though it denied any close relationship with government authority. These two private agencies were used by C.P., and it was only through Havas that the French-language papers were able to receive reports in French. Carlton McNaught refers to a survey made of British, American and Canadian dailies in 1937.[3] It showed that the Canadian papers carried a generous proportion of foreign news, with the French-language papers having a higher percentage of Canadian news and emphasizing American news, while the English-language ones carried more items from the U.K.

In *McKim's Directory* for 1937, only *La Patrie* advertised that it was a member of C.P., A.P. and Havas. Both French-language papers gave credit to the agencies for reports from Spain. The *Winnipeg Free Press* always mentioned the source of foreign news, the *Gazette* sometimes and the *Globe and Mail* very rarely. The last two papers always named the writer if a staff or C.P. staff writer. As a conservative paper, the *Gazette* relied greatly on reports from William Carney, the pro-Rebel *New York Times* reporter.

In addition to the source of news reports, there is always the question of rewriting, which might account for some variation in the news in the French-language papers. Warren Breed's Study, "Social Control in the Newsroom: A Functional Analysis,"[4] leaves open to some doubt the effectiveness of policy control in a newspaper with a reasonably imaginative reportorial staff. However, in a study of Washington correspondents, Leo Rosten suggested that most journalists may in fact find their own level and simply work for papers that suit them.[5] One would hope this is true, for declared editorial policy is not as objectionable as subtle slanting of the news in controversial fields. All these qualifications must be remembered when using newspapers as an historical source.

II

Hostilities opened July 17, 1936. The Montreal *Gazette's* first comment appeared on July 21st: "The situation as far as it can be judged, raises a very grave note of interrogation, whether he [Azana, Prime Minister of the Republic] can win today against the revolutionary and his accomplices, civil and military, in the defence of Spain's progress, as

"(6) Two leaders of the rebel forces in Seville, southern headquarters of the Fascists, leaving a military conference. General Francisco Franco, in supreme command in the south is shown in the left foreground. With him is Lieut-Col. Tague, of the Spanish Foreign Legion." *Toronto Star*, August 25, 1936. Metropolitan Toronto Library Board photo.

the Madrid government conceives progress."[6] On August 12th, the *Gazette* found it peculiar that Azana should say the Loyalist forces were weak, when there was compulsory military service in Spain and the Rebels started more or less in a haphazard way. This statement is hardly borne out by the facts, as stated in Chapter 1, which must have been known by then.

On August 26th, a correspondent in Europe reported that the Rebels were expected to win, and a final editorial on August 31st gave the reasons for the *Gazette*'s attitude. Socialist leader Prieto had blamed France and Britain for not helping the Spanish government: "He says parts of Spain would have to be collectivized after the war, so the Moderates stand to lose no matter what happens."[7] The *Gazette* was not interested in supporting a government where the Moderates would lose out after the war was over.

Even before the Civil War broke out, the *Globe* felt that the "arrival of Communism" (the Popular Front) in France, Spain and Belgium was a good explanation for Britain's middle-of-the-road attitude:

If Britain were to lean towards France the immediate interpretation would be that she was seeking to bolster up Communism. Yet Britain is committed to resist aggression and if she is to honor that commitment she may be compelled to support Communism. The alternate course would be to forget it and join the forces of Fascism.[8]

"Un groupe de recrues loyalistes reçoivent des instructions sur la façon de manier un fusil à Guadar-rama." *La Patrie*, August 19, 1936. National Library of Canada/ NL-15925.

On July 23rd, we read that if the left groups succeed, "the revolution may hasten what it was designed to prevent, the establishment of a Communist dictatorship. If the rebels win, a military dictatorship is certain at first, their plans after that are not known."[9]

By August 1st, concern is expressed about "the unprecedented action of Madrid authorities in arming the untrained masses of the people, workers, peasants, and children running wild with rifles and machine guns."[10] The *Globe* was indignant about the "material aid" pledged by political organizations and radical unions. The International Ladies' Garment Workers union had given $5,000 and a "voluntary subscription" of half of one percent of workers' monthly wages was being collected from Russian workers.[11]

The editorial of August 6th reminds us of the early position taken by the paper:

It is the partisan nature of the issue that has tied Britain's hands and restrains her from accepting or assuming leadership. The issue is between Communism and Fascism. In her own mind there is little to choose between the two. Yet to take the initiative and support one or the other would show favoritism and suggest personal motives.[12]

The *Globe* went on to say that democracy must not turn its back on the arena, but it feared that settlement of the struggle would not add much to the security of whatever democracy remained in Spain. So these two newspapers, the *Gazette* and the *Globe*, searched for a rationale to justify their support for British non-intervention policy and their fear of war and of Communism.

"LES AMAZONES ESPAGNOLES FONT LE COUP DE FEU. Des groupes de jeunes filles s'organizent pour la défense de la capitale." *La Patrie*, August 14, 1936. National Library of Canada/NL-15925.

In the early part of the war, *La Patrie* was given to screaming headlines which greatly exaggerated the text of the reports, its pages filled with photographs like the one entitled, "Amazons Fight for the Loyalists," and with little regard paid to accuracy. For instance, we are told on July 20th that the monarchy has been restored and on August 13th that "the monarchist flag floats over all Spain."[13] *Le Devoir* seems to have been more rational in its approach, if we compare two news items based on the same Associated Press report:

> Cent Prêtres sont alignés et fauchés à la mitrailleuse. Toutes les églises de Barcelone incendiées. Des enfants vêtus de chemises rouges ont fusillé des prêtres. Ces enfants étaient âgés de quatorze à dix-sept ans.
>
> – *La Patrie* [14]

Des Britanniques que la révolte a fait sortir d'Espagne disent qu'ils ont vu dans les rues de Malaga de jeunes garçons en chemise rouge fusiller nombre de prêtres et de fascistes.

– *Le Devoir* [15]

Again, on August 17th, *La Patrie* laments, "Du sang, encore du sang, toujours de sang. Tel est le mot d'ordre des nouveaux Dantons." This seems a less detached view than the report in *Le Devoir*:

> D'après une communication qui n'a pas de caractère officielle, le Vatican estime à cent soixante-deux le total des églises, chapelles et couvents incendiés en Espagne. Quelques unes des chapelles incendiés étaient dans des palais de nobles.[16]

Religieuses chassées par les troupes

Religieuses escortées en dehors de leur couvent, à Madrid, après en avoir été chassées par les soldats du front populaire.

"Religieuses escortées en dehors de leur couvent, à Madrid, après en avoir été chassées par les soldats du front populaire." *La Patrie*, August 12, 1936. National Library of Canada/NL-15926.

This photograph appeared in the *Toronto Star* the previous day with the caption "SAFETY FOR SPANISH NUNS – As intense fighting draws closer to Madrid, capital city of Spain, nuns are being ordered to leave their convents for safer regions under the care of armed guards."

★ ★ ★ ★ ★ ★ ★ ★ ★ ★ ★ ★ ★ ★ ★ ★ ★

La force aérienne d'Italie prête à entrer dans le conflit

Vue d'une partie de la force aérienne de l'Italie que l'on estime être composée d'environ 3,700 avions. Chacun de ces appareils se trouvant sur le sol italien a été mobilisé sur un ordre de Mussolini qui, affirme-t-on en certains milieux diplomatiques, aurait l'intention de s'en servir pour aider la cause des rebelles espagnols au cas où la France épouserait celle des loyalistes.

Entre temps, un compromis franco-italien de non-intervention a été élaboré et n'attend plus que l'acceptation de ses clauses par les puissances. D'un autre côté, l'Angleterre, à l'exemple de l'Allemagne, vient d'avertir les belligérants rebelles et loyalistes qu'elle est prête à répondre par la force si ses navires marchands sont bombardés, accidentellement ou non.

La Patrie, August 22, 1936. National Library of Canada/NL-15922.

Despite the violent headlines, *La Patrie* did not appear to be overly involved in the war. The editorials are on such subjects as "la simple vie rurale" and why maple syrup sells for more in Ontario than Quebec. In fact, there was not one editorial in either French-language paper at this time on the Spanish Civil War. Concern was shown, however, over whether Canada would intervene as she had in the First World War: "Le Canada sera-t-il entraîné à nouveau dans les querelles européenes? Le gouvernement King n'a pas trouvé encore le moment propice pour faire une declaration."[17] This headline was accompanied by a large photograph entitled, "La Force Aérienne d'Italie prête à entrer dans le conflit." It is an aerial photo of an estimated 3,700 Italian planes which, the paper asserts, will join Franco if France helps the Loyalists.

Both Allen Guttmann and Hugh Thomas refer to a survey made of public opinion in the United States. In it, 39 percent of Roman Catholics were pro-Nationalist as compared to 9 percent of the Protestant sample. However, 30 percent of Roman Catholics were Loyalist supporters, despite the stand taken by the Church's hierarchy and its own press.

The percentage of Roman Catholic Loyalist supporters would be infinitesimal in Canada, judging by the French-language papers I examined.

There appears to have been little difference between the views held by French- and English-language Roman Catholic papers concerning the Spanish Civil War, judging by the leading English-language organ, the *Catholic Register*. In his book on J.E. Atkinson, editor of the *Toronto Star*, Ross Harkness relates how two reporters on the *Register*, formerly with the *Star*, attacked the *Star* for its support of the Loyalists, stating that its reports were false. "If anything," an editorial declared proudly, "the *Catholic Register* has been more emphatically anti-Red than other Catholic weeklies."[18] As part of its campaign, the *Register* threatened to call for a boycott of the *Star* by all Roman Catholics on the grounds that it was a Communist paper.

Guttmann felt that some U.S. Roman Catholics wanted to affirm their loyalty to the liberal democratic tradition in the United States, and cites John F. Kennedy, who wrote home from Spain in 1937 that the government was in the right, morally speaking.[19] Canadian Roman Catholics did not seem subject to the same pressure.

III

During the next period of the war, in which the Battle of Madrid was the pre-eminent dramatic event throughout November and December of 1936, it became clear that the attitude of Joseph Kennedy, John F. Kennedy's father and U.S. Ambassador to Great Britain, was a stronger force than the liberal democratic tradition in determining U.S. policy. At first, the United States had no law covering shipment of war materials to countries engaged in civil war and used a "moral embargo." But an attempt to break the ban by shipping aircraft engines to the Spanish government resulted in a bill forbidding all exports of that kind. It passed both houses with only one dissenting vote.

By November the Fifth Regiment based on the Communist-Socialist Youth had been organized and the International Brigade arrived in Madrid on November 12th. Both events raised the morale of the untrained Spanish troops, and all the European powers were amazed that Franco was unable to take Madrid and end the war. Britain led the way in producing mediation, non-intervention and volunteer plans, all of which were futile.

On November 9th, the *Gazette* believed the outcome of the battle was not in doubt, and hoped Madrid would be the decisive battle. However, it stated:

It does not follow that Franco's victory will be more than an episode in the revolutionary evolution of the country or that he can organize the changes that must ultimately come in Spain. It will remain to him and his more enlightened supporters to demonstrate an ability to control and govern the crowd of reactionaries that surround them.[20]

After previous editorials one would not expect to read on November 25th that, while Communism was "infinitely the lesser of two evils, there is no alternative but a strict policy of neutrality or an already tense situation would be aggravated."[21]

On December 1st, Madrid is described as a new city compared to Toledo and Granada: "Madrid will be newer still after the defenders and besiegers are through with their destructive fighting. It will have to be rebuilt."[22] An editorial that reflects William Carney's anti-Loyalist reports from the *New York Times* stated that isolated war is horrible enough, but it would be much worse if other countries were drawn openly into the fray. On December 21st, we are reminded, "it has been stated often in these columns that the cure for Communism is prosperity."[23] Further down the page we see that "a constant harping on the prospects of war will tend to make the risks all the greater. The situation is not bad enough to mar the enjoyment of the 30-day Christmas holiday of [British] Members of Parliament."[24]

The last *Gazette* editorial of the year concerning the war was a long one, about the possibility of shipment of planes from the U.S. to the Loyalists: "Congress should deal with this immediately after it meets next week. The planes will take some time to be put into shape. Perhaps Congress will enact amendatory legislation that will stop them."[25]

The *Globe and Mail* shared that opinion, saying that it was hard to be neutral about the loophole in the United States' neutrality legislation. It seemed willing to advise Britain, as well as to follow her lead, stating that Britain should not "act in a way that could be interpreted as sympathetic to the Rebels or, for that matter, the Leftists."[26] Blum had been urged by radicals to give up the non-intervention agreement, a resolution duplicated by the British Labour Party, but, said the *Globe and Mail*, "Britain won't yield to pressure at home or abroad:"[27]

British citizens would do well to remember that their espousal of either Fascist or Communist principles, though undertaken solely with the purpose of fighting the rival "ism", must have the effect of weakening the Empire and of undermining democracy in favour of some form of despotism.[28]

However, the *Globe and Mail* did not consider all British ideas worthy of support, among them Lord Marley's suggestion that the "anti-fascist" Council of Civil Liberties in Great Britain be copied by Canada:

He discriminates in selecting the foes of democracy. Why is the organization not Anti-Communist too? In Marley's mind, fascism may be the greater threat in Great Britain. At present Communism is much more potent as a trouble maker in Canada, Fascism was unheard of till Communism became dangerous to European "liberty".[29]

"TERROR STRICKEN BUT STILL DEFIANT, CITIZENS OF MADRID RESIST STUBBORNLY. (1) Women and children carrying pitiful bundles of personal belongings, fleeing from the bombarded areas." *Toronto Star*, December 11, 1936. Metropolitan Toronto Library Board photo.

As James Eayrs states in his article, "A Low Dishonest Decade: Aspects of Canadian External Policy, 1931-39," "totalitarianism was thought to be merely an aggravation of that malaise from which Europe traditionally suffered. The fascist apparition was no new menace... it required no special explanation; created no new problems; needed no exceptional precautions."[30]

The *Globe and Mail*'s confidence in Britain rarely weakened: "No one can guess what form international strategy is taking. Britain and France are sincere but the others play along to be diplomatic."[31] While Hitler might "attempt to strike down Czechoslovakia or march armies into Spain there is one

"(2) An unshaven prisoner, captured by the rebels during a raid upon Madrid, awaits his fate at the hands of his captors." *Toronto Star*, December 11, 1936. Metropolitan Toronto Library Board photo.

other factor beside the danger involved which can prevent further action. It is that British diplomacy has made Hitler see reason."[32]

Le Devoir had developed more partisan feelings by this time and reprinted many articles from anti-Communist organs, containing such alarmist statements as, "On dit déjà qu'une armée de 500,000 hommes [Russes] va être mise sur pied equippée et armée de la façon la plus moderne."[33] On November 11th, we read that the attack on Madrid is progressing very slowly because "Franco tenait à limiter au minimum les ruines."[34] The longer Madrid held out, the fewer reports from the front and the more reprints of stories of atrocities committed by Loyalists appeared in *Le Devoir* and *La Patrie*.

One could not expect anything else from the French-language papers, if a speech by the Reverend William Bryan, S.J. was typical of the Church's attitude: "D'un côté se trouve le communisme avec tout ce qu'il represente, de l'autre tout ce qui s'oppose au communisme."[35] The issue, he said, was not, as the Communists portrayed it, democracy versus reactionary forces, or liberty versus fascism, or the Roman Catholic Church versus Communism. After all, he warned, there were very few fascists behind the Rebels, whereas in Montreal there were 800 members of the Communist Party and 30,000 sympathizers.

Although *Le Devoir* stated that the British were supporting both sides, with General O'Duffy and 40 Irish volunteers fighting for the Rebels at Burgos, it could not say how many British were fighting for the other side.[36]

IN MADRID — A street scene in Madrid as householders dragged their furniture from homes threatened by rebel bombs and shells

Toronto Star, December 17, 1936. Metropolitan Toronto Library Board photo.

A very significant headline on December 22nd read: "Franco établit un conseil superieur de guerre. Les autorités militaires d'Espagne appellent sous les drapeaux la classe de 1931 pour la 'phase finale' de la guerre."[37] The Rebels, it would appear from the headline, now constitute the military authorities of Spain.

As usual, *La Patrie* emphasized photographs, of buildings in Madrid, both intact and in ruins, and of

refugees and exhausted fighters. On November 6th, a headline proclaimed, "Franco sera dictateur, l'homme à la bonne humeur contagieuse, mais à la main de fer."[38] On November 6th, it would appear that all hope of saving Madrid from surrender has been lost, but on the 16th a commentator on the editorial page found that "Madrid est ce que les Americains appellent 'a hard nut to crack.' "[39] Unlike *Le Devoir*, *La Patrie* carried few reprints, but shared

A family look at their belongings on a Montreal street following their eviction during the Depression. National Archives of Canada/C-30811.

its sympathies in an editorial on the war, a rare event in a French-language paper: "De quel côté en Espagne se fait la guerre juste? . . . La charité chrétienne nous commande, certes, d'aimer nos ennemis et de prier pour eux, elle ne nous commande pas de favoriser leur victoire."[40] Moreover, according to *La Patrie*, outside powers had recognized the junta of Burgos, which is portrayed as representative of law and order and the Spanish mystique.

Allen Guttmann says that, while most of the mass circulation papers in the United States were against Franco, the Hearst ones and many magazines favoured the Rebels. Of these, some, including *Time* and *Newsweek*, became Loyalist supporters after the bombing and defence of Madrid. No similar change of position occurred in Canadian newspapers, as we have seen, nor did any occur in April and May of 1937, following the attack on Guernica.

Red Atrocities---Read All About Them!

LEONARD WALSH

THE reactionary Canadian daily press is still winning the Spanish civil war for the Fascists. When the constitutionally elected Madrid government finally drives its enemies with their Mohammedan mercenaries and German-Italian armaments into the Mediterranean Sea, it will be over the prostrate and bleating forms of the Montreal *Star* and *La Presse,* Quebec's *L'Action Catholique,* the Toronto *Mail and Empire* and the *Catholic Register* . . . to name only a few of the worst offenders.

Not that pro-Fascist propaganda disguised as news is limited to the press of Montreal and Toronto. From the Maritimes to the west coast "red-atrocity" stories are splashed in the boldest Gothic type, emanating from such unbiased points as Lisbon, Rome, Seville, and the shifting location of the Fascist headquarters. A few papers are living up to their liberal traditions by printing news reports from unbiased and even pro-Government sources, but their headlines are pale waifs beside the black banner lines of those who ache to see another Fascist state in Europe.

The technique of discrediting the Spanish people in the eyes of Canadian readers is exquisitely simple and includes these easy steps:

1. For the benefit of those who read only headlines, the latter are made to present the blackest case for the Government forces, or to suggest that they are as good as beaten. Example, the Montreal *Star* of August 28, exclaims "REBELS REPORT MASS EXECUTIONS . . NOTABLES AMONG MANY SENTENCED . . . MADRID SITUATION DESPERATE." The close body type reveals that the *Star* is featuring another Fascist-inspired "atrocity" story, and that the "desperate" Madrid situation consists of "a Rebel broadcast . . . asserted that Extremists had killed 2,000 persons there in two nights."

2. All the old gory descriptions of outrages on clergy, nuns, novitiates, churches, women and children, that so effectively whipped up hatred of Germany during the last imperialist war are revived. Most of these anecdotes hail from Spanish Fascist headquarters, where imaginative rebels fill full time jobs devising them. As often as not, the source of the atrocity story is buried in type if not dropped altogether. "FIVE HUNDRED PRISONERS OF MADRID CHAINED AND CAST INTO THE SEA", "SPAIN PLUNDERS THE CATHOLIC CHURCH", "FIENDISH ATROCITIES BY REDS IN SPAIN" are choice items. The last is by the Toronto *Catholic Register,* H. Somerville, editor. "50,000 FREED CRIMINALS RUNNING AMOK IN MADRID" screams the Montreal *Star* for August 28.

3. The device of labelling Spanish Government forces Reds, Communists, Anarchists or rabble, is employed.

4. So is that of quoting the word rebel, so: "rebel". The trick of rejecting the word Fascist altogether and substituting *Patriot!* This latter ingenuity is consistently practiced by *L'Action Catholique* of Quebec City and by the *Catholic Register.*

5. The above are amplified by the ruse of minimizing stories of atrocities committed by Fascist forces on Loyalist prisoners and civilians which have been broadcast not only by Madrid, but by the Fascist radio stations themselves! This includes the practice of writing editorials on the outrageous conduct of the Government militia in editions that carry tucked among the advertisements, stories of outrages committed exclusively by the Fascist aggressors.

6. The deliberate falsification of news.

Scan, briefly, the front page headings of *La Presse* from July 28 to August 27, for a full month of iniquity. The first lead is emphatic: "SPAIN PLUNDERS THE CATHOLIC CHURCH". On August 1, contrary to all fact, *La Presse* readers were advised that "THE REBELS ARE AT THE GATES OF MADRID". August 3 the keynote was "ANTI-CHRISTIAN TERROR IN SPAIN". On the 12th, great joy! "THE REBELS HAVE TAKEN SAN SEBASTIAN". (San Sebastian weeks after is still a Loyalist city). On August 18 "TRUCE AT SAN SEBASTIAN" is "RUMOURED" and on the 20th, "ROME DESPAIRS OF NEUTRALITY". On August 22nd it announces "GREAT REBEL ASSAULT ON MADRID" following it on the 24th with the lie that "ALL THE SPANISH NAVY REBELS". On the 26th "MADRID IS ON THE DEFENSIVE EVERYWHERE". August 27th effects

13

New Frontier, October 1936, Metropolitan Toronto Library Board photo.

LA BLESSURE

this gem, "LOYALISTS PRETEND THAT MOORS IN REBEL SERVICE ARE MUTINYING".

L'Action Catholique does not lag behind. On August 26, when reports of the failure of a major Fascist drive had found their way into most English-language papers, this pro-Fascist paper declared "THE PATRIOTS ARE VICTORIOUS ON ALL FRONTS". (For Patriots read, as noted, Fascists). Subheads added, "They are advancing slowly on Madrid to avoid regrettable destruction. Segovia is in the hands of the patriots. Madrid takes urgent measures to organize the defence of the capital. It seems that the last phase of the Spanish civil war has started today." This argument is furthered by the Halifax *Herald* of August 25 which insists that the "(SPANISH) PRESIDENT PREPARES TO QUIT MADRID". For contrast, the events of the fatal August 26th were honestly reported by the Kitchener *Record* (among other papers), "REBELS BLOODY OFFENSIVE FAILS TO ACHIEVE GOAL". On the same date, however, the Windsor *Daily Star* would have it otherwise with "REBELS SMASH LOYALIST LINE".

But the *Catholic Register* is the true playboy of the pro-Fascist press. Most of the front page of the August 27th issue convulses with hate for the Spanish people defending themselves against the forces which boast they will establish Military Dictatorship, annihilate all republicans, loyalists and their sympathizers, "even to the extent of fusilating half the population of Spain". (See the formal Manifesto from Rebel Headquarters of August 27th). Under the banner "FIENDISH ATROCITIES BY REDS IN SPAIN" the *Catholic Register* catalogues alleged "atrocities": "At Barcelona 150 young seminarians were lined up and shot", "reds in besieged cities try to protect themselves by threatening to kill hostages if patriotic forces attack them", "shootings, crucifixions and burnings alive", "Passionist and Franciscan communities massacred". Previously the *Register* has screamed "Red forces in Spain losing ground", "Russia's hand behind Spain's troubles", "Priests are hunted", "Sacred host outraged", "Red Vandals", "graves of nuns horribly desecrated" and the like. The immediate issue proceeds: "The Patriotic forces of Spain, wrongly called rebels, are

steadily overcoming Red resistance. The nominal Government in Madrid is not regarded as a real Government by any Government in Europe, except Russia; it is merely a figurehead for the violent rule of Anarchists and Communists". This is a flat lie, naturally, as the Madrid Government has every recognition. From this premise, a curious Jesuistical deduction follows: "The French Government is a 'Popular Front' Government and the French Premier is a Socialist, yet the French Government has taken the lead in proposing an international agreement to ban the supply of arms to either side in Spain. As the pro-Reds in Canada and elsewhere urge in their complaints against France, it is unprecedented for any Government to forbid the supply of arms to another Government faced by rebellion. *The answer is that the civil war in Spain is not a conflict between Government and rebels*". Then the paper gets down to the business of the day: "There are reports of crucifixions in several places. It is reported that in Madrid five Carmelite nuns were crucified by women anarchists. A priest escaped from Taragona says that to appear on the streets wearing a hat or necktie was to invite instantaneous death as indicative of membership of the hated wealthy class".

Willie Hearst and Lord Rothermere can both sit profitably at the feet of the talented staff of the *Catholic Register*.

The surprising thing about it all is, not that papers from coast to coast have been butchering the news to make a Fascist holiday, but that there has been so little protest from it from their readers. In both Great Britain and the United States, committees of well known writers and intellectuals have signed public letters to the most reputable newspapers, demanding that they print the truth about Spain. That this action has had results can be seen by reading back copies of the London *Times*, which quickly changed its editorial tone after receiving a letter of protest from prominent intellectuals. Similar action here in Canada might also bring results, but there seem to be none who will take the initiative in lending their name to a movement for an unbiased press. Meanwhile, those who really want to know what is going on in Spain read the liberal and radical periodicals and the labor papers.

LA PRESSE

TRAHISON

IV

In March 1937, Franco turned to the north and launched an attack on Bilbao and the Basque provinces. The Republic had considered this front less important than the south, and the Communists disliked José Aguirre, President of the Basque Republic, and his independent followers. No one could question their bravery under fire, and the subsequent attack on Guernica aroused sympathy in many countries.

Guernica, a town of 7,000 people near Bilbao, was the symbol of Basque liberty, for it was before her famous oak that the Spanish monarchs had customarily sworn to observe Basque local rights. On April 26, 1937, a market day, the town was bombed for four hours, and people fleeing from it were machine-gunned. It was the first aerial attack on a civilian population in history. Approximately 1,600 people were killed and 900 wounded. Both the Nationalists and the Germans denied any involvement, but in 1946 Goering admitted that Guernica had been a testing ground for aerial attack.[41] Reporters in the town at the time were able to send accurate news of the bombing, and on April 28th, the *Gazette* carried G.L. Steers' detailed report on the attack. But the *Gazette*'s only editorial concerning Europe at that time was in praise of Blum for his efforts to remedy the genuine grievances of the working class in France.

The *Globe and Mail* carried the headline, "Basque Horror Laid to Nazi Flyers" on April 28th, but all its editorials that week dealt with Reds in the C.I.O. The letters to the editor concerned subjects like the "Sundays of Long Ago" and "Jack Flown Upside Down when Presented to the Baltimore Orioles." On May 5th, there was an indignant protest about the claim of a Chicago agency that British policy had changed to a pro-Loyalist course:

> Britain and France are taking refugees out of Bilbao because of Guernica within their rights as neutrals. Franco is angry about this not because it is an intrusion on behalf of the Loyalists, but because it implied belief of his guilt in the Guernica charges.[42]

However, late in May, a long article by J.V. McAree appeared on the editorial page stating that the charges arising out of Guernica were too clear to be termed Red propaganda, as in the past:

> Franco has lied copiously and industriously from the beginning, but those who pointed this out were in danger of being denounced as Reds. Franco has an advantage in the matter of propaganda, because the foreign correspondents with his army are under strict control, going only where permitted to go under escort."[43]

On April 27th, *La Patrie* carried the headline, "Ville Espagnole en Flammes, Centaines de Morts,"[44] but did not identify the aggressor. Rather, a comment on the editorial page on April 30th harped back to the atrocities committed by the Loyalists: "A leur tour les loyalistes espagnols affirment que les insurgés ne cessent de commettre des cruautés. Ces recits d'atrocités deviennent monotones."[45]

With the idea that a French paper outside of Montreal might have a different view, I looked at *Le Droit* of Ottawa for this period, but it was similar to its counterparts in Quebec. Covering a speech by Mme. Anna Louise Strong on the attack on Guernica, *Le Droit* said she must obviously be a Socialist since she defended the Communists and anarchists who had created the reign of terror in Spain. The story goes on to defend Franco: "Les nouvelles à ce sujet sont contradictoires et le quartier général des troupes blanches en répudie la responsabilité en ces mots 'Aguirre ment, l'Espagne de Franco n'allume pas incendie. Nous avons respecté Guernica . . . Basques, déposez vos armes, confiez-vous à la justice de Franco qui a serenité et noblesse.' "[46] Evidently it did not seem incongruous to *Le Droit* to carry below its report of Mme. Strong's speech an article on the terrible treatment that Roman Catholics were receiving under Hitler in Germany. Hugh Thomas tells us that two prominent Roman Catholics, François Mauriac and Jacques Maritain, had issued a pro-Basque manifesto that spring. Guttmann speaks of U.S. Catholics also being troubled by the attack on the devout Basques. No such compunction was expressed in the papers of French Canada.

V

The last period I examined, from January 25th to the end of February 1939, covers the fall of Barcelona, the flight of Spanish refugees into France and

FAVORS
INSURGENTS

BESIEGED SINCE
OCT 2, 1936

FRANCO BROUGHT
REVOLT HERE
JULY 19, 1936
FROM CEUTA

INTERNATIONAL
ZONE

FRANCE

SAN
SEBASTIAN

BILBAO • IRUN

ANDORRA

TREMP •

ZARAGOZA •

BARCELONA

PORTUGAL

GUADALAJARA •
MADRID

TOLEDO

CASTELLON

VALENCIA

BALEARIC IS

LISBON

ALICANTE

SEVILLE •

CORDOBA •

CARTAGENA

SEA

GRANADA •

MEDITERRANEAN

CADIZ •

GIBRALTAR

ALGIERS

TANGIER •

CEUTA

SP. MOROCCO

AFRICA

0   50   100
MILES

LOYALIST TERRITORY

With the Catalonian capital now fallen into the hands of the enemy,
territory still occupied by loyalist forces is indicated by shading in
this map.

Toronto Star, January 26, 1939. Metropolitan Toronto
Library Board photo.

the recognition of Franco's government by France
and Great Britain.

Both the *Gazette* and the *Globe and Mail* were by
that time aware of the menace posed by the presence
of Germany and Italy in Spain, and published an
increased number of letters on the subject, although
the views varied greatly. One published in the *Gazette*

on February 1, 1939, argued that since Moscow
interfered in the affairs of Spain, Germany and Italy
had a right to step in. The following day, a well
written letter strongly defended the Loyalist cause
in replying to a priest who had said: "If the Spanish
Loyalists win, the victory will be Russia's, while if
Franco's armies win the Spanish people will be the

A crowd of family and friends wait in the Montreal station to greet the returning volunteers, February 1939. National Archives of Canada/C-67452.

victors."[47] The writer says she is not for or against any "ism," which is rather contradicted by her final paragraph: "You say the American people detest Communism and are convinced they are clever enough to manage their own affairs. If so, why all the anti-Communist propaganda? A country will get the kind of government it deserves, the Russians have been trying to work out their own salvation ever since the Revolution and have succeeded wonderfully."[48] The letter is signed, "Perplexed, St. Joseph, Quebec." In rural Quebec in 1939, a Communist supporter might well have been perplexed.

One interesting *Gazette* editorial says relief cannot be general at the war's end while Italian troops remain in Spain. This "cannot but strengthen the impression that the so-called Civil War was in reality more a war of conquest by foreign troops than anything else."[49]

Two days earlier, on February 5th, crowds in

Montreal had cheered the returning members of the Mackenzie-Papineau Battalion, themselves embittered by the odds stacked against the Loyalist side. Montreal Mayor Camillien Houde had been forced to refuse quarters to the Mac-Paps in Atwater Market when his Council charged that they were Communists. On February 8th, the *Gazette* reported on Mayor Houde's speech at a Y.M.C.A. dinner, where he referred to French Canadians as Fascists who had always been under dictators such as Louis XIII, Richelieu, seigneurs and priests, and who had always been followers of one man, whether Papineau, Cartier, Laurier or Lapointe. These remarks indicate the volatile and warm-hearted mayor's aversion to his Council's attitude.

An editorial on February 17th described the horrors of war, with its subsequent retribution and refugees, and proclaimed it

"On n'avait plus d'armes à nous donner"

Un volontaire canadien qui combattit dans les rangs loyalistes d'Espagne, arrivé à Montréal, hier soir, raconte au reporter de la "Patrie" que les volontaires ont été licenciés parce que le gouvernement espagnol n'avait plus d'armes à leur donner. H. Herman Anderson, de Winnipeg, se trouvait ce matin aux bureaux des "Amis du bataillon Mackenzie-Papineau". *(Photo la "Patrie")*.

La Patrie, February 13, 1939. National Library of Canada/NL-15922.

...a marvel any sane person would stand for any leader who advocates armed conflict. Yet some attack Chamberlain for his policy of appeasement. Do they wish to make other people undergo the terrible experiences that Spain is going through?[50]

The *Globe and Mail* appears to have changed its line slightly or to have become more defensive about it at the end of the war. On January 25, 1939, we read: "Democracy still has a chance. Men who should be giving leadership to a united front talk neutrality and plot impractical schemes for avoiding involvement."[51] A few days later, an editorial comments, "there is nothing to be gained by carrying on the struggle, nothing but more destruction, misery and hardship for the Spanish people. Intervention if not too late has become more difficult than ever and many times more dangerous from an international viewpoint."[52]

The return of the Mackenzie-Papineau Battalion was front page news. The returning men blamed the lack of arms and equipment, which would have enabled them to win, on the arms embargo. On February 22nd, a letter was published denouncing the paper's hypocrisy: "if the *Globe and Mail* is sincere in its oft-repeated protestations of democracy, it would use editorial space to condemn the embargo which allows Franco to receive supplies and the Loyalists nothing."[53] Meanwhile, the *Globe and Mail* was devoting much of its energy and space to a newly created Leadership League.

Le Devoir carried a long editorial entitled "De Barcelone à Ottawa" on January 27th: 'France and England are worried about a foreign influence in Spain but Franco has denied the possibility. Suppose it did come to war, do you think Canada would have to enter the struggle? If you think this ridiculous, remember last September when we nearly did this, under the pretence of preserving Czech democracy, in reality for the safety of English interests. So it is not strange to link Ottawa and Barcelona, be on guard!' *(author's translation)*.

In a column of comments on the editorial page of February 28th, the question is asked, Why don't all the refugees go to Russia where they belong? Another comment is rather smug on the defeat of the Loyalists: "Les gens du poing tendu sont knockout. Franco leur a mis le point final."[54]

The French-language papers appeared to be more interested in a victory for Roman Catholicism than worried about foreign influence in Spain. *La Patrie* actually ran two editorials on the fall of Barcelona, the Holy City of Loyalist Spain, the anarchists' and workers' stronghold so feared by the Nationalists:

La capture de Barcelone n'est pas une victoire totalitaire mais espagnole . . . Vous avez vu des Catholiques basques prendre parti pour les forces soviétiques. Tout arrive en ce bas monde et le cynisme s'ajoute parfois au mensonge. Par bonheur les Chrétiens ont une guide qui voit de haut les événements. Le Pape s'est franchement ouvert à M. Chamberlain de ses sympathies envers Franco. N'ayons crainte: L'homme s'agite et Dieu le mène. C'est le Christianisme qui vainc, par Franco, l'athéisme rouge.[55]

Completely at odds with the editorials are two articles in *La Patrie* by Albert Duc.[56] He spent two days with Canadians who served with the Loyalists and gave his impressions of the men in his long and sympathetic accounts. These men, he said, belonged to all parties and religions and were objective in their views: "Ils furent des soldats, ni plus, ni moins." He quotes George Edgar, at 55 the oldest in the battalion, who describes the war as "comme une vaste laboratoire où à peu près tous les pays du monde ont fait l'essai de leurs armes nouvelles." One of the accompanying illustrations shows a valueless German mark obtained from a Moorish soldier and comments that, while the Germans and Italians were properly paid, the Moors received cigarette coupons and Confederate money as pay.

It is difficult to understand the publication of these articles in the context of what has gone before. They are definitely inconsistent with the previous attitude we have seen in all four newspapers, which relayed a fear of involvement in foreign wars and, above all, a hatred of Communism either for religious or economic reasons. Perhaps the French-language reporter had a greater tradition of freedom of speech than was found in the English-language newspapers. Perhaps, with Franco's victory, the Red menace was less threatening than it had been.

— Et maintenant, je viens "travailler" en France...
(Gringoire, dessin de A. R. Charlet).

La Patrie, February 18, 1939. National Archives of Canada/C-27802.

VI

It is evident that the viewpoint of these publications was strongly influenced by fear of Communism. It is interesting how often the conservative papers accused Spain of being Communist even before Russia intervened since, when war broke out in 1936, there were only 14 Communist deputies in the 600-member Spanish Cortes. This sentiment had a religious basis for the French Canadians and an economic one for the English Canadians, epitomizing the ideas of "survivance" and "the Protestant Ethic." Isolationist feelings were omnipresent, although the English-language papers concentrated on Britain's lead in drawing back from the conflict, while in the French-language papers Britain's position was not a factor.

Facist tendencies were public and visible in Quebec during this period, with Adrien Arcand, leader of a major Fascist organization, claiming to represent 80,000 members. Although the English-language papers express-ed their aversion for 'Republican anarchy' in terms of a desire for law and order, Arcand was described by the *Globe and Mail* as "the brilliant young French Canadian"[57] in a series of articles on Fascism, and *Maclean's* magazine ran a two-part series on him. At the same time, *New Frontier* quoted Ross McMaster, a Montreal industrialist, as saying that democracy was not the system of government for times like these.

Franco's disciplined supporters backed by army, church and the establishment had always appealed to the right, and so it is not surprising to find support for him, tacit and explicit, in the mainstream newspapers. As George V. Ferguson has said in his article on "Freedom of the Press":

The newspaper of free western society began as a function of the free enterprise system, it has never been anything else and remains a stronghold of that system to this day . . . . Ownership of the press does rest in the hands of the rich and well to do and opinions expressed in it are, broadly speaking, right wing in character.[58]

CHAPTER 3

"Spain is a scar on my heart"

Spain is a scar on my heart. Do you understand? It is a scar that can never heal. The pain will be with me always, reminding me of the things I have seen.

– Dr. Norman Bethune[1]

Understandably, many of the publications that gave strong support to the Loyalist cause were not owned by supporters of free enterprise. Their backgrounds and reasons for supporting the Republic varied greatly, ranging from Communist through Socialist to Liberal and Labour viewpoints. Yet they all believed that the Spanish government, as the legal, elected government, deserved support from the League of Nations and from other countries. They gave extensive coverage of the tour of a delegation sent by the Spanish government to raise funds in North America, and raised objections to military material and supplies from Canada reaching Franco. This chapter will cover the newspapers. The periodicals will be discussed in Chapter 4.

The *Winnipeg Free Press* and the *Toronto Star* were anomalies among major newspapers I examined in that they supported the Loyalists. The *Winnipeg Free Press* was rather a maverick. Liberal in ownership, it was influenced by its milieu, where the heritage of the Winnipeg General Strike was still strong. Wilfred Kesterton told me that in 1936 the *Toronto Star* was nearing the end of its most sensational period. Its many promotional schemes had resulted in a circulation of 243,217. The editor, J.E. Atkinson, supported socialist beliefs and saw Fascism as a menace to the world.

II

The editor of the *Free Press* from 1901 to 1944, John Dafoe, a Manchester Liberal, made the newspaper the spokesman of the Canadian West; on occasion, the paper's editorial policy was contrary to the ideas of the publisher, Clifford Sifton. According to Kesterton:

> In a situation virtually unique in Canadian journalism Dafoe had a bargaining position far stronger than is generally realized, so that Sifton's behaviour was probably not quite as altruistic as sometimes believed . . . The geographic, ethnic, and economic character of Winnipeg acted for the paper's catholicity of interests.[2]

J. King Gordon believed that Dafoe's position on Spain was "consistent with his belief in collective security and the League of Nations, with his deep distrust of Britain and his persistent criticism of Mackenzie King's isolationism. Moreover, for thirty years he had fought the big interests represented by the Montreal *Gazette* and the *Globe and Mail*" (*personal communication*, 1969).

In 1936, Winnipeg had a Socialist mayor, John Queen, and Communist aldermen like Jacob Penner, while a Communist, Jim Litterick, sat in the provincial parliament, his huge popular vote reflecting strong labour support, much of it from workers with a radical European background. The *Free Press* is listed in the 1936 *McKim's Directory* as Independent

ELIMINATION BOUT FOR THE CHAMPIONSHIP OF THE WORLD

Toronto Star, July 24, 1936. Metropolitan Toronto Library Board photo.

Liberal with a circulation of 60,802. There were many foreign-language publications within the city, including Ukrainian, Russian, Jewish and Hungarian ones.

In an editorial very early in the war, the Rebel uprising under Franco is clearly presented:

> In Spain then, the Socialists are "red" and the "left Republicans" not far from it. Two of the principal acts of the Leftist Government since February have been the release of 30,000 political prisoners and the suspension of rents payable by tenant farmers pending parcelling out of the big estates. It is against this radical regime that the royalist, military and Fascist groups are trying their strength in armed rebellion. They have one legitimate grievance, in the February election the rightist parties got 54% of the votes but less than half the seats in the Cortes.[3]

This is the most unbiased newspaper report I have seen at the opening of hostilities. It admits that the government represents a minority of the popular vote, but states unequivocally the basis of Franco's support – dislike of the revolution in land tenure. Many papers ignored the real issue, and concentrated on the violence and anti-religious bias of the Loyalists.

The same month in Winnipeg, L. St. George Stubbs, a former city judge and a Socialist, received the largest number of votes in the provincial election in his constituency. He was considered the voice of the oppressed, having been dismissed from the bench after deciding the case of a disputed will in favour of charitable institutions and against the family of the deceased. His popularity and that of Jim Litterick and Mayor Queen are important in understanding the Loyalist support seen in letters from readers of the *Free Press*.

On August 8th, the paper advocated support for the Republic by shipment of arms:

> The Rightist rebellion has no colour of legality about it as an attempt to unseat a usurper might have. Technically then, other European powers would be right in permitting the shipment of arms to the government of Spain, wrong in allowing their nationals to give any aid to the Fascist cause. This is the view taken by the United States government in the American Civil War, but international law gets very little respect in Europe in 1936.[4]

An even stronger editorial appeared later in the month, criticizing the non-intervention pact in no uncertain terms:

> The Spanish government holds office by lawful authority, the others are like a gang of pirates. Italy and Germany aid a breach of international law, but the democratic nations are too afraid of war to intervene on the side of law, therefore they propose neutrality. Two powers in Europe are getting ready for war, the powers that want peace have no policy.[5]

On November 2, 1936, we see a story on the reception of the Spanish delegates in Canada. Isabel de Palencia, Spain's diplomatic envoy to Sweden, Marcelino Domingo, Socialist and former Education Minister in the Azana government, and Father Luis Sarasola, a Basque priest, came to North America on a speaking tour to tell of the Loyalist plight and gain support for the Spanish government.

In order to understand the uniqueness of the *Winnipeg Free Press*'s coverage, it is necessary to backtrack somewhat. On October 23rd, when the delegation arrived in Montreal, the headline in the *Gazette* had declaimed, "Local Diocese warns Catholics against Spanish Loyalist Priest." The civic authorities feared a riot at the meeting, which was scheduled to be held at the Arena, as both students and Fascist groups were already threatening to make trouble. The meeting was sponsored by the Committee for Medical Aid to Spain, and the arrangements committee was headed by Professor Frank Scott, who denied that the speakers were Communists.

Under Quebec law, most meetings were illegal unless held with a police permit. After much discussion among city officials and police, Alderman Savignac, Chairman of the City Council, refused to grant a permit, saying, "We will not allow Communism to take root here." At the same time, a meeting for students had been arranged under the auspices of the Social Problems Club of McGill University. Because threats to break up the meeting had been received, precautions were taken and students guarded the entrance to the McGill Union (the liberal student centre). The meeting was well attended with no disturbances.

"EMISSARIES OF SPANISH LOYALISTS IN TORONTO ON SPEAKING TOUR OF CANADA AND UNITED STATES. (1) The emissaries as they arrived at the Union Station. They are from LEFT to RIGHT: Father Sarasola, Senora Domingo, Senora Palencia, member of the Spanish national committee against war and Fascism; and Senor Domingo, president of the left republican party in Spain and former minister of education." *Toronto Star*, October 20, 1936. Metropolitan Toronto Library Board photo.

Refused the use of the Arena, Professor Scott tried to move the meeting to Victoria Hall, where he was told all space was rented, although the main auditorium was dark that night. Another plan to move the meeting to the Mount Royal Hotel was frustrated. According to Professor Scott:

Democracy is in a precarious condition if a sane and considered statement for a lawful government is prevented from being given in a British colony by threats of violence from irresponsible elements. The three delegates are travelling on diplomatic passports and have held meetings in Toronto, Ottawa and Hamilton.[6]

All the Montreal police force were out and 2,500 students, released from school in order to make trouble according to Professor Scott, paraded around town, searching for a meeting that failed to materialize.

Throughout the weekend sporadic demonstrations continued – the office of a local newspaper, a bookstore, the home of a member of the CCF, and the McGill Union – were all damaged or received written threats. On the Sunday, the Feast of Christ the King, 100,000 Roman Catholics assembled to hear "a denunciation of communism and a call to all the faithful to join a crusade for its extermination. Canadian support of Spanish Loyalists – 'those barbarians who have covered the soil of unhappy Spain with ruin and blood' – was denounced."[7]

In Toronto, the delegates held a meeting but did not receive a civic welcome, in spite of the protests of the *Toronto Star* and various organizations. Instead, the delegates were greeted by hundreds of people headed by the Reverend Ben Spence. The *Star* carried several photos and articles on the delegates and the meeting. They spoke at Hart House at the University of Toronto in the afternoon and went on to a civic welcome and meeting in Hamilton that evening. One writer in *Saturday Night* said that, as liberty and free speech were important to him, he

Hamilton City Council Permits Tag Day To Aid Doctor In Spain

Special to The Star

Hamilton, Nov. 11.—With four members dissenting. Hamilton city council yesterday gave permission to "women in Hamilton banded together to aid Spanish democracy to hold a tag day on Saturday to raise funds to aid Dr. Norman Bethune, Canadian doctor now assisting women and children in Spain."

"We are just butting our noses into someone else's war and I object to our citizens being tagged to aid one side of warring factions," stated Alderman Evans.

"Dr. Norman Bethune is recognized by the Canadian Red Cross and he is the only Canadian doctor there," stated Controller Nora-Frances Henderson.

"Why need we go so far from home for causes for mercy?" asked Alderman John Marsh. "If I were asked for a tag day here to aid our own needy, I would be told that our welfare agency did that, and I would be refused. Yet our own community fund is not supported."

"Spain's government is the constitutionally elected, democratic type we are proud to be acquainted with," observed Ald. Agnes Sharpe.

"There are different types of government going under the name of democracy," observed Ald. Elliott, adding, "In our land, one of our highest ideals is the taking of the oath of allegiance, and tribute to the flag. Some members of this council have not done that."

Toronto Star, November 11, 1936. Metropolitan Toronto Library Board photo.

would have acted as a special constable for Father Luis if he could have had "ordinary people and not a pink professor on each side of him."[8] Evidently, even Socialism was too strong stuff for this man.

Given Montreal's turmoil and official Toronto's snubs, Winnipeg's welcome must have surprised and pleased the delegates. On November 3rd, the *Free Press* reported that 2,500 people met them at the station. This issue contained two pictures of the crowd, one of the delegates and one of the welcoming committee of prominent citizens. There are some surprising names on the list, which includes Mayor John Queen, Marcus Hyman, MLA elect, Alderman Margaret McWilliams (whose husband was Lieutenant Governor of Manitoba at a later date), J.S. Woodsworth and Mrs. Woodsworth and Joseph T. Thorson, MP.

Alderman McWilliams entertained the delegates at breakfast that morning and Mayor Queen gave a luncheon for them at the Royal Alexandra Hotel. So many people came, it was necessary to hold two meetings; Mayor Queen was chairman at one and

Hon. B.J. McMurray, K.C. at the other. Donations included $500 from the Russian people of Canada, $300 from Jewish organizations and $100 each from the Workers Benevolent Association and the International Ladies' Garment Workers.

When interviewed in January 1969, Mr. Justice Thorson remembered the circumstances of his presence at the station when the delegates arrived in Winnipeg. He had spoken in favour of the repeal of Section 98 of the Criminal Code in the 1935 election, arguing that it would be wise not to make martyrs of Communists, but to let them state their case and then defeat them. Thorson, running for the Conservatives, had defeated a Communist candidate in the 1935 election and said that his presence at the station was the result of his interest in and objection to Section 98. While he was at the meeting addressed by the delegates, his wife received a phone call advising her to get him away from the meeting, as they were all Communists. To quote him, "Not all at the meeting were Communists, but misguided people who wished to help the Spanish government."

"(1) A platoon of women soldiers drilling in Madrid before going into the battle lines." *Toronto Star*, October 21, 1936. Metropolitan Toronto Library Board photo.

(3) *Toronto Star*, October 21, 1936. Metropolitan Toronto Library Board photo.

CIVILIAN WORKERS TAKE UP ARMS IN MADRID

Civilian workers from every occupation have taken up arms in Madrid, led by the exhortations of the women of the capital as the sounds of artillery in action reached the city. Commanders tried every possible means to obtain conveyances to rush the civilian volunteer army to the battle lines in an attempt to hold the rebel advance. The pictures here show: (1) A platoon of women soldiers drilling in Madrid before going into the battle lines. (2) Loyalist militia marching out of Madrid to meet the advancing rebels. (3) A banner strung across a Madrid street reading: "They shall not pass. Fascism is attempting to conquer Madrid. Madrid will be the tomb of Fascism."

As well as a lengthy report on the meeting, the *Free Press* carried an article initialed G.V.F. on the editorial page on November 3rd. In it, the writer presented the events of October 23rd in Montreal as a question of free speech and civil liberties in Quebec:

> Fascist blackguards in Montreal with the active assistance of the civic authorities and the tacit approval of the Roman Catholic Church were successful in preventing their [the delegates'] appearance at any public meeting in the largest city in Canada. According to Mayor McKenna, "so long as I occupy this chair there will be no meetings held in Montreal under Communistic auspices. I hope that is quite clear?"
>
> "Do you think anybody who contends that the present Spanish loyalists are not Communists can be classed as a Communist on that account?" he was asked.
>
> "Yes, I do."
>
> "Do you class McGill professors who were injured in Friday's troubles as Communists?"
>
> "Some of them I do. And I think they ought to know better."
>
> This is a good sample of official Montreal thought at the present time.[9]

Professor Frank Scott told me that many years after the war, he visited Senora de Palencia who was living in Mexico. He did not need to see the crucifix in her room to be convinced that she was not a Communist.

The *Vancouver Province* gave a favourable report of the arrival of the delegates:

> One thousand persons stood beneath the crossed flags of Canada and the Spanish republic and cheered to the echo four delegates of the beleaguered Spanish Government. It was a remarkable demonstration of sympathy for the democratic cause in Spain.[10]

However, such an attitude was not typical of all Southam papers in the west, for the *Regina Leader Post* showed no support for the Loyalists from August to December 1936. On November 3rd, when the Spanish delegates were in Regina, the *Leader Post* said both sides of the question should be heard, but carried no report of the meeting they addressed that evening.

On November 5th, a *Vancouver Province* news item reported that the militia formed in Winnipeg to aid Spain had disbanded, as the Single Unemployed Men's Association had decided to wait until it heard from Prime Minister W.L. Mackenzie King. There had been 1,000 applications from Alberta, Manitoba and Ontario, all from men with military training. The Association opposed King's farm placement scheme, evidently preferring to go to Spain. However, by December 21st, we read that the single unemployed men were wise to take the farm jobs, and that 30,000 had been placed in the Prairie provinces. This was another triumph for Mr. King's policy of wait and conquer, for the legal position of Canadian volunteers for Spain would soon be a delicate question for the government.

On November 9th, the *Free Press* issued a clear statement on its position, a more realistic approach to the conflict than that seen in many Canadian newspapers:

> Assisted by the Fascist governments of Germany and Italy, in flagrant violation of international law and of the non-intervention agreement, the rebels have gained steadily in recent weeks. The government was a duly elected government, though the left-wingers in office were not immediately successful in restraining the murderous element among Spain's radicals, their social purposes were, on the whole, admirable. Their aim was to make Spain a modern nation through popular education, abolishing special privileges and raising the economic level of the peasants.[11]

In the crucial period November and December of 1936, all the newspapers carried more news about Spain than at any other time, and the *Free Press* was no exception. Many letters appeared, arguing about Father Sarasola and the atrocities committed against the clergy, until the latter subject was closed for discussion. There was a very informative series of articles on the Communist Party by a former member, giving names, dates, etc. Publishing these in a civic election year drew an angry blast from Communist candidates in the election.

Here is a sample of the wide variety of items about the Civil War published in the *Free Press* during this period. The stories of a Winnipeg airman home from flying for the Rebels were reported without comment. He was sure Franco would win,

SPANISH WAR STRONG MAN INTERVIEWED BY FREDERICK GRIFFIN

In the CENTRE of this group, wearing riding breeches and puttees, is General Emil Kleber, known in Toronto, Austrian by birth, but Canadian citizen by naturalization, commander of the international troops fighting the rebels from Madrid. Kleber was interviewed by Frederick Griffin of The Star staff, only Canadian newspaper man in Madrid. Mr. Griffin described this colorful person as the strong man of the Madrid defences. He is shown chatting with a group of members of the British parliament during their recent tour of the various Spanish war sectors.

Photographs of this group appeared in other newspapers and in *The Spanish Civil War* by Hugh Thomas. *Toronto Star*, December 16, 1936. Metropolitan Toronto Library Board photo.

---

and asserted that any atrocities had been committed by the Loyalists, since the Rebels were too well disciplined, although they took no prisoners. In a report from the other side on November 28th, under the headline, "Canadian Named as Leader of Madrid Defense Army," we read of General Kléber, who came to Canada as a child, served in the Canadian army in World War One and became head of the International Corps. According to Hugh Thomas "Kléber was built up by Communist propaganda to be a soldier of fortune of naturalized Canadian nationality."[12] This is the description applied to him when he is shown in a picture in the *Free Press* with British members of Parliament in December 1936.

In the same month, the *Free Press* was accused by a reader of championing Communism in its zeal for democracy. Its response was that it had used only reputable news services and that articles had been published with complete impartiality as received. (It has already been noted that the *Free Press* acknowledged the source of its news reports more than most other newspapers examined.) It quoted the *London Times*, which had said "that the ruthlessness of the insurgents is as revolting as any of the cruelties perpetrated by supporters of the government."

The *Free Press* wondered why the most avowedly patriotic sections of the British public desired the Rebels' success, which would be a threat to Britain's power in the Mediterranean. The writer decided that it was "all due to mania arising from class sentiment and property sense."[13]

WINNIPEG, FRIDAY, MAY 7, 1937.

"COME ON IN, I'LL TREAT YOU RIGHT. I USED TO
KNOW YOUR DADDY."

—C. D. Batchelor, in the "New York News."

This cartoon won the 1936 Pulitzer prize, an award given for
a distinguished example of a cartoonist's work published in any
American newspaper during the year.

FOR BETTER OR FOR WORSE?

Toronto Star, January 26, 1939. Metropolitan Toronto Library Board photo.

Winnipeg Free Press, May 7, 1937. National Archives of Canada/C-27803.

No *Free Press* editorials appeared on the subject of the attack on Guernica, but one on May 1, 1937 attacked British foreign policy for not supporting the League of Nations.

The return of the Mac-Paps in February 1939 was, of course, covered in detail. They were welcomed at the Winnipeg station by 4,000 people. Among the speakers were Jim Litterick and L. St. George Stubbs, who said, "The humblest one of these boys is more entitled to a royal welcome than the King and Queen because of what they have done individually in the cause of democracy."[14] Many Ukrainian names appeared on the list of veterans, including the son of the Chairman of the Ukrainian Farmer Labour Temple Association of Canada. A mass meeting chaired by Professor Osborne of the University of Manitoba passed a motion against the non-intervention policy and censured Premier Bracken, and especially Mayor Queen, for not being at the station or on the platform. In this respect Winnipeg resembled other cities where officials were not on hand to greet the returning volunteers.

The final editorial on Spain repeated the case the *Free Press* had presented often before:

Recognition is the logical consequence of the policy followed in both London and Paris, a policy over which this newspaper has expressed its dismay not once but many times . . . The civilized world has watched a truly republican government being beaten into the ground by reactionary insurgents, helped by aid from countries which violated an agreement, and in so doing international law was flouted.[15]

The *Free Press* was a Canadian newspaper with a large circulation and an independent editor. Exposed to Communist and radical European influences, it took a broader view than most other major newspapers. Its writers seemed able to describe the situation on both sides and point out the flaws in each one.

Letters published were a kaleidoscope of readers' opinion covering a wide range of belief and personality, while the editorials could quite easily have appeared in the Socialist press.

III

In 1936, the *Toronto Star* was an afternoon paper representing both middle- and working-class opinion. Its coverage of the war in Spain included editorials, articles, many photographs, and special series from their reporters on the scene, such as Matthew Halton, Pierre van Paassen and Frank Pitcairn. Letters from readers concerning the war frequently appeared in the "Voice of the People" column. The paper's radio broadcasts requested letters received from Spain, so that news of the situation there could be shared with others.

In light of all this, the first editorial on the war seems strangely neutral:

> The Fascist revolt in Spain and Spanish Morocco aims at the restoration of the monarchy. The Spanish situation is confusing because the working classes have little respect for the Parliamentary system which they have found to be corrupt and inefficient. This has encouraged Fascists to seize power by force, but for reasons of their own, the peasants and workers are rallying to the aid of the hard-pressed government.[16]

The July 29th issue carried Matthew Halton's interview with Francisco Largo Caballero, leader of the Socialist party. In London for an international conference of trade unions, Largo Caballero spoke of the necessity for European democracies to form a united front with Russia. If not, he said, they would all be locked in battle with the Fascist dictators before 1940.

On August 5th, Pierre van Paassen, European correspondent for the *Star*, described terrible scenes of death and fire in Barcelona. A Loyalist supporter, he carried a stretcher on this occasion and he wrote that the Fascists set the churches on fire: "I saw them do it," he said. The issue of August 7th contained a wide range of opinions about the war: van Paassen described Fascist atrocities; the editorial stated that, in the long run, the policy of neutrality might be much the best for the hard-pressed government of Spain; and W.D. Euler, Minister of Trade in Canada, felt that Hitler was seeking trade, not military victory.

On August 8th, "Voice of the People" carried an interesting letter from the Municipal Workers Union in Moscow to a Toronto union official asking for information on the life and work of municipal workers in Toronto and promising to send similar material in return – an early *glasnost*. Two days later, Alice Chown praised the *Star*'s editorial on neutrality, and asked people to support the International Peace Conference. She named several women who would be attending from the League of Nations Society.

The August 20th editorial pointed out an unusual feature of the war in Spain:

> The rebels are accorded, internationally, the same status as the government of Spain. Karl Marx said the real issue is always the class issue. As someone has said, the war in Spain is between the palace and the hovel, and most countries sympathize with the occupants of palaces.[17]

Photos of Pierre van Paassen and his wife Coralie appeared on August 25th. She had mailed his 18 articles on Madrid from Paris and was off to the French-Spanish border to report on conditions there. The August 28th editorial states that "Britain and France will pay dearly for their desertion of Democracy – unprincipled weakness seems to characterize the free peoples of the world."[18]

On August 29th, we read, "If Germany and Italy keep their neutrality pledges, the Loyalists with greater material resources should be able to overcome the advantages given to the rebels by their trained fighting personnel and superior equipment."[19] The views expressed in the editorials may have been intended to maintain the *Star*'s impartiality. On August 31st, when a letter stated that all news from Spain was Fascist propaganda, the editor replied, "Mr. Case should have excepted the *Star* from this charge."[20]

The Battle of Madrid began on November 8, 1936, and was one of the strangest in modern warfare. A well-equipped army but one of only about 20,000 men, mainly Moroccans and legionnaires, engaged in a fierce struggle against an ill-armed but huge urban mass.

By November, Russian tanks had arrived in Spain, and Germany had promised powerful reinforcements, if they were placed under a German commander and if Franco would see to it that the war was "more systematically and actively conducted."[21] Franco agreed, and the Condor Legion was as-

"Husband and wife are covering the developments in Spain and on the French frontier for Star readers – Pierre van Paassen (7) The Star's European corres-pondent and his talented wife, Coralie van Paassen (9)." *Toronto Star*, August 25, 1936. Metropolitan Toronto Library Board photo.

sembled at Madrid with Colonel Richthofen as Chief of Staff. According to Thomas, this force comprised a battle group of four bomber squadrons of 12 bombers each, a fighter group of the same strength, and a seaplane, reconnaissance and experimental squadron. It was supported by anti-aircraft and anti-tank units, and two armoured units of four tank companies of four tanks each. There were 6,500 men in the Condor Legion.

The Germans wanted to see the civilian reaction to an attempt to set fire to the city, quarter by quarter, and concentrated the bombing on hospitals and other important buildings. This new form of warfare created a vision of the tank and bomber as images of doom. However, Madrid did not surrender. Masses of workers left for the front lines, a women's battalion fought in battle, and children helped to build barricades.

An editorial entitled "Canada does not want war" praised Prime Minister Mackenzie King's speech on this topic at Geneva. On the following day, the front page headline read "Madrid is doomed," but in an interview by Matthew Halton, Norman Bethune reported that Madrid was amaz-ingly calm, though the defenders faced execution if they lost. On November 7th, a letter signed "Fair Play" defended Britain's foreign policy, "as our own government and, I believe, no one else in Canada would go to war against fascism."[22] Tim Buck, leader of the Communist Party in Canada, had just returned from five weeks in Spain. He understood that the Second World War had already begun there, and was very impressed by the confidence and great spirit of the common people in Spain.

On November 12th, Frank Pitcairn, the young English correspondent from the *Daily Worker,* who served as a militiaman at Madrid, compared the onslaught to the relatively equal combat when the Civil War began: "Now men with old rifles are facing the newest bombing planes in the world."[23] Halton sent back a series of articles from the area around Madrid and the paper carried many photos of devastation in the city. The November 19th editorial described the war as "a struggle of the many against the over-privileged few and their foreign hirelings," who "are making an inferno and a slaughterhouse of a great city."[24] It also pointed

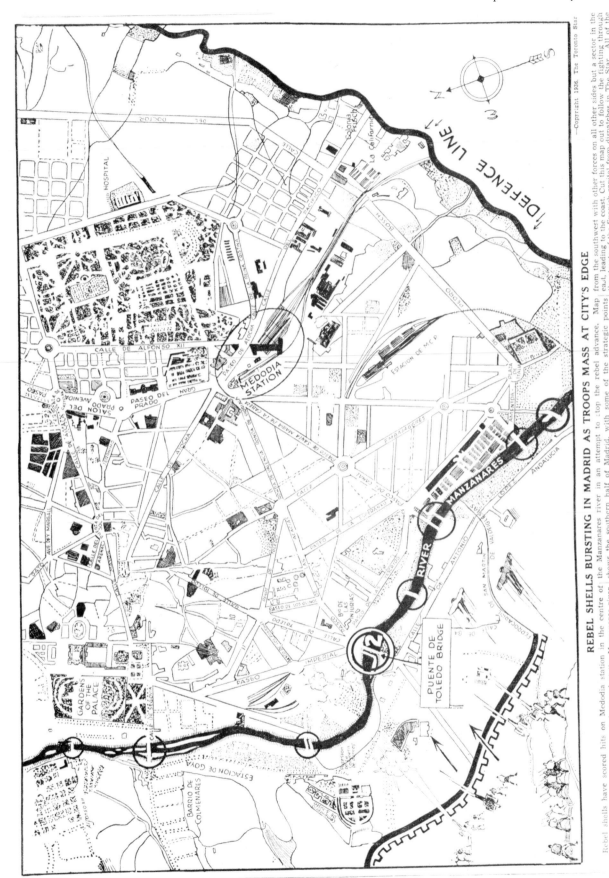

Toronto Star, November 7, 1936. Metropolitan Toronto Library Board photo.

Frederick Griffin of Toronto Star In Ruined Madrid

REBEL BOMBS SHATTER MADRID—Frederick Griffin, Star special writer, is in the Spanish capital, Madrid, now the scene of terrible devastation as rebel shells and bombs take their toll. LEFT: Firemen fighting a blaze in Madrid caused by an incendiary bomb. RIGHT: Loyalists crawling among ruins of San Sebastian church in the heart of Madrid

Toronto Star, December 5, 1936. Metropolitan Toronto Library Board photo.

out that international law granted arms-importing privileges to a lawful government. The previous day's editorial had asked why the Loyalist troops were not better equipped. The answer is obvious: Franco's army had all the weapons, and no democratic country, despite international law, would sell war materials to the Loyalists.

A November 28th headline read, "Once Toronto citizen has strategic post in Spanish Capital," referring to General Emilio Kléber, supreme commander on the northern Madrid front. The same issue contained a photo of Frederick Griffin, a writer for the *Star* for 20 years. He was travelling to Europe on the Queen Mary to write a series on the war.

By December 2nd, the heaviest battle of the war had resumed in Madrid. On the 5th, Fred Griffin,

On May Day, 1937, the Communist Party of Canada pledges unity between the workers of Canada and Spain. National Archives of Canada/C-74966.

"the first Canadian in the city," wrote that the city was still standing and calm. In fact, one could take a street car to the edge of the war zone. One-quarter of the population had been evacuated, there was no heat and little food, but discipline was good. Planes had attacked a hospital and a prison area to clear the way for Rebel troops. Franco was ready to announce the capitulation of Madrid on December 8th, the Feast of the Immaculate Conception. On that date, Griffin visited the Garibaldi Battalion, part of the International Brigade. He did not see how Franco could take Madrid, except foot by foot. He also reported that General Miaza had received a letter to protest the bombing of the city from Canadian professors, ministers and doctors.

On December 12th, Griffin told of meeting Kléber, whom he described as "a cross between Max Schmeling and Fritz Kreisler." Born in Austria,

Kléber had fought in Siberia and with the Russian and Chinese armies. One news story reported that he had worked for the Communist Party in Toronto. When Griffin questioned him, he replied, "Do you know Tim Buck? Ask him, he knows all about me."[25] Although his Canadian background was open to question, his ability as a general was never doubted.

Meanwhile, back in Toronto, the Canadian Corps Association reported that Communism was being taught in the back rooms of Toronto cafés. The *Star* wrote, "Colonel R. Hill suggested the organization of a vigilante committee. 'I think we can have some fun one of these nights.' His listeners applauded."[26] Reverend F.D. Sholin, who had been a missionary in Spain before his recent return to Toronto, was interviewed on December 18th and said that his sympathies were entirely with the government,

IN MAY DAY PARADE TO QUEEN'S PARK FOR MASS MEETING

One of the first groups to arrive | paraders to Queen's park for the | Hungarian girl workers with thei
at Stanley park to join the May Day | mass meeting was this group of | banners.

Toronto Star, May 1, 1937. Metropolitan Toronto Library Board photo.

which had never been a threat to his People's Church.

A December 21st editorial characterized the war as "not a Spanish war but a European class war involving Fascists, Anti-Fascists and adventurers."[27] Christmas Eve's issue printed two poems by Constance Davies Woodrow. Here is the first verse of "Christ in Spain, Christmas, 1936":

You of the thorn-crowned head and stricken face,
Where will you stay?
Not in this whole wide land is there a place
For you today.[28]

On December 29th, Halton reported that the British embassy had been closed and Britons told to leave Spain. In his opinion, the Spanish Anarchists were the true democrats. At this time, two major news stories filled the Toronto papers – the abdication of King Edward VIII and the conclusion of the infamous Millar Stork Derby. (Ten years before, an eccentric Toronto millionaire had willed $500,000 to the Toronto mother who bore the most children in the next decade.) Nevertheless, the *Star*'s coverage of the significance of the British gesture was extensive.

Surprisingly, the *Star* contained a story but no editorial on the attack on Guernica. However, on April 29, 1937 a headline which read "McGill head's failure to curb 'pinks' held reason for resigning" made the front page. In 1936, Chancellor Edward Beatty of the CPR had made a speech hinting at ing, that production here and in other countries has far outgrown the science and politics of economics, or economy. In the past we have restricted distribution and earning power in order to maintain prices. Money has been issued in the form of credit based upon the value of goods which cannot be sold.

If we knew how to make it possible for everyone to earn surplus goods and service without enforced employment by the government, there would be a more real democracy, and plenty for all, within reasonable limits.

EDMUND T. NESBITT
24 Tyndall Ave.

NOT SATISFIED
To the Editor of The Star.

Sir: Prime Minister Mackenzie King finished off his speech on the floor of the House recently with these words: "I shall seek to serve this country in the best way I can according to the best light my conscience can give me." Looking back over the past ten years, do the social conditions in Canada here bear the evidence of conscientious leadership from Ottawa? Our young unemployed men have been obliged to sleep in box cars at nights and wander the highways by days. In Montreal a single unemployed man or woman receives the sum of $1.80 per week to clothe, feed and otherwise keep body and soul together. Our only hope is that some new group will move into power very soon. J. C. JONES
Montreal, Que.

AN APPRENTICESHIP SYSTEM
To the Editor of The Star.

Sir: Ten years ago I had the opportunity of studying the English home service apprenticeship plan. I

which is today being persecuted in countries where justice is being replaced by brute force, and civilization and religion are menaced by savagery and paganism.

D. D. BLOOM
168 Bloor St. W.

THE LOYALISTS OF SPAIN
To the Editor of The Star.

Sir: May I utter a word of appreciation in regard to your editorials on the Spanish civil war. You have put the blame and responsibility squarely where it belongs, on the shoulders of Mussolini, Hitler and Franco and the governments of Britain and France who, blind to their own dangers if Franco and his foreign confederates win, allow a brave and freedom-loving people led by a people's government to be crushed. Fighting to the bitter end against overwhelming odds, it would seem at the present moment as though the cause of freedom and democracy must suffer eclipse on the blood-stained soil of Spain.

Almost surrounded, with food supplies running perilously low, the gallant defenders of imperilled democracy are resolved to die fighting rather than yield to the despoilers of their hearths and homes and the dictator-controlled invaders. With the great democracies headed by Chamberlain and Daladier weakly yielding to Hitler and Mussolini, no wonder we hear the wish expressed, "O for an hour of Cromwell, Canning or Gladstone!"

If Britain, France and the United States had acted firmly and promptly to check Japan, Italy and Germany when they first threatened to seize their neighbors' territory the unspeakable tragedies that have been enacted during the last eight years might have been avoided. N. L. SWART

LIKES "THE VOICE"
To the Editor of The Star.

Sir: Each issue of your paper is better than the last. The editorials have covered a wide range of subjects and dealt with them in an able manner. The Voice of the People column is most interesting. In Tuesday's Star, Jan. 17, I find a letter signed by Margaret Addison which is indeed a first-rate letter, in which the writer displays an unusual insight, genuine, original thought, and wisdom made still richer by learning, and above all a power of appealing to inner sentiments which all feel yet are reluctant to express.

I know something of communism from observation of what it has accomplished in a few years for an illiterate herd of human beings whose condition is still bad but infinitely better than ever before. I have found that capitalism produces millionaires and bread lines, I can see that the unearned wealth of the idle rich is only matched by the unmerited poverty of the workers who serve.

With regard to socialism I know very little except that it is proving a great blessing in Sweden. I also know a Gallilean Carpenter who was its very first exponent. If, then, we find by experience or study that our present system with its stubborn insistence on private competitive profits obstructs progress and the functioning of the service motive, let us have the vision, initiative and courage to displace it with a system of planned production that can and will translate into fact and reality the service standards of Jesus.

WILLIAM T. FOLEY
Belleville, Ont.

MODERN SONGS
To the Editor of The Star.

Three interesting letters typical of those that appeared in "Voice of the People" during this period.

Toronto Star, January 21, 1939. Metropolitan Toronto Library Board photo.

---

curtailment of the right of professors to teach certain economic theories. Principal Morgan, a defender of freedom of speech, had expressed satisfaction that the McGill students had stood for an elementary civil right in holding a meeting to hear the Spanish delegates. His position had incurred the wrath of the governors of McGill.

A very successful May Day parade was well reported. As May 1, 1937 fell on a Saturday, thousands marched to Toronto's Queen's Park, where a meeting was held. Fifty unions were represented by contingents, and one float represented an ambulance for Dr. Bethune. Many adults wore red and white caps and carried banners showing support for Spain's

Popular Front government. One photograph showed the crowd at the meeting, and another featured a group of young Hungarians in red-and-white outfits with a sign supporting the women of Loyalist Spain.

On May 3rd, Margaret Gould, former Secretary of the Toronto Child Welfare Council and author of a series of excellent articles for the *Star* on Russia, interviewed Anna Louise Strong, who had just arrived in Toronto from Spain on her way to the U.S. Gould spoke Russian and had spent some time there the previous year. Strong had gone to Russia as a social worker with the Friends Relief in 1920. She married a Russian writer, stayed in the country and published a book titled *Spain in Arms* (New

FRANCE

60,000 MORE LOYALIST TROOPS EXPECTED IN FRANCE

97 MISSING CANADIANS FOUND AT PORT BOU

40,000 LOYALIST TROOPS FLEE TO FRANCE

ANDORRA
LE PERTHUS
PERPIGNAN
SEO DE URGEL
PUIGCERDA
Figueras
PORT BOU
GERONA
Vich
CATALONIA
Lerida
Cervera
Fraga
CALDETAS
Barcelona
Reus

0   50
MILES

LOYALISTS STREAM INTO FRANCE FROM DOOMED CATALONIA

Before the steady onslaught of Franco's insurgents, loyalist troops and refugees poured over the Spanish-French frontier today in ever-increasing numbers, leaving Catalonia to the enemy. At least 20,000 troops surrendered their arms at the border and crossed into French territory before noon. An additional 60,000 government soldiers were approaching the frontier. Premier Negrin of loyalist Spain and cabinet members have retreated to French soil, hoping they can return to defend territory still held by the government in central Spain. From Port Bou came the report today that 97 Canadian members of the international brigade, unlocated for several days, had remained to fight instead of joining their comrades in returning home.

Toronto Star, February 6, 1939. Metropolitan Toronto Library Board photo.

York, 1937). She compared the Loyalist government to the Roosevelt one, saying that the common people had united to elect both.

Gould asked her about a collective farm 900 miles east of Moscow set up by 80 Canadians and Americans 15 years before when it consisted of 700 acres. Strong reported that it had grown to 14,600 acres and was run by an international group. They were also using a new method of feeding farm workers by bus – the predecessor of the coffee van.

By the winter of 1938-39, food was in appallingly short supply in the Republic. The Rebel attack launched on Catalonia in December moved very quickly and the Nationalist army entered the city of Barcelona on January 26th. Air raids were continuous and refugees in the city were estimated at one million.

A strong editorial on January 27, 1939 criticized the French and British governments for surrendering valuable ground and betraying principles and friends in their dread of war. By January 28th, France would only admit non-combattants. After 16 inches of snow fell on the road over the mountains, hordes of men, women and children staggered into France. One week later, 250,000 Republican soldiers laid down their arms and were allowed to enter. Few countries wished to take the refugees, and conditions in France's refugee camps were deliberately primitive.

On February 2nd, a reader thanked the *Star* for "its splendid editorials and articles which it features on behalf of freedom, democracy and social reform."[29] The first of several long, sympathetic articles about the return of the Mac-Pap Battalion appeared on February 3rd under the heading, "Shabby War Scarred Canada's Beau Gestes come marching home." About 300 volunteers had arrived in Halifax on the Duchess of Richmond. Their leader, Edward Cecil-Smith, son of an Anglican bishop, pointed out that their battalion had been

Stealthy Goers-Forth to War Who Came Loudly Home

William Fodey, RIGHT, of Toronto, a devout Catholic, shows his friend, E. B. Rose, a trapper of Cold Lake, Alberta, the bright mulberry Spanish mantilla he is bringing home to his wife. These two men were comrades throughout much of the fiercest fighting in Spain, and Fodey comes home wounded in the shoulder and abdomen

Bruce Ewen, 21-year-old, is joyously greeted by his Toronto sister, Isabel, but he has another sister, Jean, serving somewhere in China. Isabel lives on Beverley St.

Toronto Star, February 6, 1939. Metropolitan Toronto Library Board photo. (*Note:* Jean Ewen, author of *China Nurse 1932-1939*, worked with Dr. Bethune in China.)

WELCOME

The Fighting "Mac-Paps"

Canadian Volunteers Returned From Spain

HEAR

Major Ed. Cecil-Smith

BATTALION COMMANDER

and others

REV. FATHER R. H. THOMAS, CHAIRMAN

MASSEY HALL

TONIGHT 8 P.M.

DOORS OPEN 7 P.M.   ADMISSION 15c, 25c, 50c

Toronto Star, February 6, 1939. Metropolitan Toronto Library Board photo.

named for the grandfather of the premier who forbade Canadians to join it. Gregory Clarke wrote:

> These men were mostly enlisted by the Communist and other radical groups in Canada who have tried to help their comrades while Canada as a whole kept muttering, 'Tut, tut, tut.'

Some men were afraid to give interviews in case it would prejudice their chances of obtaining jobs. All "wanted to see Spanish democracy victorious and would go to war again for democracy or Canada." Fred Baxter, a World War One veteran from Fredericton said, "I went to Spain to kill as many Fascists as possible; that's all the less to kill when they get here."[30]

Gregory Clarke commented: "Their war stories have a gentle madness that reminds you of Don Quixote."[31] The volunteers had been paid 300 pesetas or eleven dollars a month. The Spanish govern-

ment had disbanded their unit in September 1938, when Premier Negrin told the League of Nations he was withdrawing all internationals in order to eliminate all doubts about the national character of the cause for which the Republican army was fighting. He also hoped this might force withdrawal of Italian and German troops.

At Barcelona, 98 of the men wanted to re-enlist but were refused, as Spain had promised to demobilize the volunteers. Here the men were given the civilian clothing put in storage by Republican soldiers when they enlisted. The Spanish government paid their fare home as far as Toronto, but the men chose to travel by steerage and colonist car to reduce the cost borne by the government. The Friends of the Mac-Paps in Halifax made 1,650 sandwiches for the trip to Montreal. The six blankets on the train went to the men in the hospital car and the Toronto "Friends" sent clothing for distribution on the train. In Montreal, a meal was provided for them in

Captain Cecil-Smith addresses a crowd in Union Station following the arrival of the Mac-Paps in Toronto, February 1939. National Archives of Canada/C-67441.

Windsor Station. Cecil-Smith reported that the CPR tried to prevent them from meeting the 2,000 people waiting to see them. They arrived in Toronto on the evening of February 4th.

On February 6th, one page of photographs showing the soldiers' reunions with their relatives and friends in Toronto illustrates the varied backgrounds and lifestyles of the volunteers. A meeting to welcome the men and raise money for medical care and financial help was advertised and held that day: The Friends of the Mac-Paps hoped to raise $50,000 to avoid the men having to go on relief. Massey Hall was almost filled, despite such short notice. The Reverend R.H. Thomas of the Church of St. Mary Magdalene was chairman and the Reverend Salem Bland of the United Church and Margaret Gould appeared on the platform, along with Labour and City Council representatives. The crowd rose and cheered for five minutes as the men came in. The American Loyalist Vets sent a cheque for $5,000, presented by Frank Rogers, political commissar of the Mac-Paps. The Spanish consul laid a wreath on the memorial altar on the stage. The *Star* later carried letters of thanks from the volunteers, and, on February 8th, an angry letter about Mayor Day's statement that the men were not eligible for relief.

An editorial on February 10th criticized the use of a British cruiser to help Franco's forces acquire Minorca as Britain had not withdrawn its recognition of the Madrid government. However, "theirs was now a hopeless struggle."[32]

When 50 more Mac-Paps arrived in Toronto, Fred Griffin wrote: "Someday it will be remembered to their glory that they served in Spain with the International Brigade of many men from many lands."[33] The February 18th issue contained a Spanish child's drawing of life in Barcelona. Brought back by a volunteer, it was on display at an exhibition of paintings, sculpture and handicrafts in the gallery of the Women's Art Association. Another day, a scene painted and contributed by Sir Frederick Banting was shown. All the pieces on display were to be auctioned to raise money for Spanish refugee children.

Franco was banking on "a place in the sun" and expected to have an army of one million men. On February 23rd, he promised Mussolini and Hitler full support in the use of Spanish air and naval bases in case of war. As war in Europe approached, fear of Italy and Germany increased. Britain was planning to add 60 battleships to her navy. The *Star* ran pictures of France's defence system, the Maginot Line, along with praise for the system's self-sufficiency and "brain centre"! On February 25th, pictures showed Madrid sandbagged in anticipation of Franco's attack.

When Britain and France recognized Franco's regime on the 27th, the *Star* commented that their action was "really a surrender of the quarter of Spain still in Loyalist control."[34] Franco, waiting to move in with food and troops after the surrender, refused to grant peace terms and denounced "the eternal Jew – whom nobody wants because they are a communist horde which advances."[35] The confused and bitter end to this tragic war reflected the major flaws the democratic countries had displayed throughout the 1930s, a weakness which ensured the outbreak of war across Europe only six months later.

ART SHOW WILL AID CHILDREN OF SPAIN

Sir Frederick Banting Among Artists Who Have Loaned Work

Donated by artists from all over the Dominion, an exhibition of paintings opens in the galleries of the Women's Art association, Prince Arthur Ave., Monday. Proceeds of the sale will be donated to the refugee children of loyalist Spain.

Many notable artists have donated examples of their work. Among them are A. Y. Jackson, Lawren Harris and Sir Frederick Banting.

Madame Paraskeva Clark is convener of what promises to be one of the most successful exhibitions ever held in the Women's Art Centre. Of particular interest is a selection of drawings by the children of Barcelona. They were made just before the city was abandoned by the loyalist troops and show the vivid impression made on the minds of the children by the daily visits of bombing airplanes and the conditions under which they lived. These drawings were brought back to Canada by members of the Mackenzie-Papineau battalion.

Toronto Star, February 18, 1939. Metropolitan Toronto Library Board photo.

LIFE IN BARCELONA IS REFLECTED IN CHILDREN'S DRAWINGS

A child in Barcelona under 14 years of age made this drawing. The red, gold and purple flag of Republican Spain flies from the truck carrying troops. The old people salute with clenched fists. It is one of a collection brought back by Mackenzie-Papineau veterans. They will be on display next week at a sale of Canadian art in aid of Spanish refugee children. The exhibition will be at 23 Prince Arthur Ave.

Toronto Star, February 15, 1939. Metropolitan Toronto Library Board photo.

CHAPTER 4

Periodicals Pro and Con

The periodicals were as varied in their views as the newspapers. *Maclean's* magazine and Toronto's *Saturday Night* took positions similar to the *Gazette* and the *Globe and Mail*. The *New Commonwealth* and the *Federationist* of B.C. represented the CCF officially, and the *Canadian Forum* represented it intellectually. *New Frontier,* published in 1936 and 1937, was much more radical.

Maclean's magazine's spokesman on the Spanish Civil War was usually Beverley Baxter, whose "London Letter" was widely advertised and read. A Canadian protégé of Lord Beaverbrook, he became a Conservative Member of Parliament in Great Britain, and he was fond of regaling his readers with accounts of life in the best circles, both town and country. At first he could not see any alliance between Italian Fascism and German Nazism, nor did he believe there would be a Great War: "Spain has sunk so low in international influence that our interest in her is almost entirely academic and historical. Yet she must be counted as a unit in the irresistible trend to the Left."[1]

Evidently Baxter echoed editorial policy, for, in December 1936, an editorial as strong as any found in the French-language newspapers appeared with photos of a vandalized church. The editorial said the Communist Party had established schools all over Canada and asked:

> Where is a school devoted to the training of youth according to the doctrine of British democratic government? These photos in the *Illustrated London News* are evidence of the wanton, hysterically violent, anti-religious sacrilege perpetrated by Left Wing Extremists in the name of Communist Democracy. . . . Properly placed before the Canadian people, the complete records of the British form of Government and of private enterprise should leave in the minds of Canadians of all classes no doubt as to which guarantees them the highest standard of living, the most liberty, the peaceful correction of whatever abuses may exist.[2]

On several occasions Baxter referred to Canadian reaction to his writing. In March 1937, he was surprised that so many readers had written asking if he would elucidate the attitude of the British government to Spain. The explanation he offered was a simple one: "the extremists swept aside a weak government after the 1935 election and proclaimed a new order of liberty, equality and murder"; however, "General Franco rose to save the old order of things, calling on God and the Moors to liberate Spain." Baxter could not understand why Germany and Italy had not informed Britain before recognizing Franco's government, but felt that the Spanish government had everything to gain by doing nothing to "aggravate" foreign influence:

> We believe in London this is a civil war, not ideological. Spain is paying for her past sins. The British Government desires the victory of neither one side or the other. A better Spain will rise, slave neither to Fascism or Communism.[3]

A true disciple of Chamberlain, he believed Ger-

"Excesses of hysterical Red 'Democracy'. An anti-clerical peasant cheerfully smashing a Madonna with a pickaxe." *Maclean's*, December 1, 1936. National Library of Canada/NL-15929.

many did not want war, and stated that Hitler was brutal, but not vicious. The following excerpt from the "London Letter" is typical of Baxter's views:

> Poor old Britain refused to plunge Europe into a gigantic war because some ex-bullfighter fired a pistol in Spain. Patiently, wisely, and honorably it drew a cordon of sanity around unhappy Spain, and, though the sparks flew high, they never ignited the neighbouring states.[4]

An article by George Drew portraying Russian Communism as a ghastly failure was illustrated with several pictures from the Spanish Civil War. It drew the response from a reader in British Columbia that the article was biased and crude: "what is wrong with Canada, if we cannot bear a comparison with the system of another country?" Mr. Baxter did not seem to realize that not all Canadians shared his views, for he wrote with some incredulity:

> Quite obviously there is a school of thought in Canada, mostly around Winnipeg, which distinguishes very clearly between Russia and Germany, (to the latter's detriment) and while professing strong loyalty to the England that was, has little use for the England that is![5]

Baxter received much more criticism after Chamberlain returned from Munich and he quotes from several letters, emphasizing, in a derogatory way, that they were all from women. Not surprisingly, *Maclean's* readers seemed to question Beverley Baxter's inaccurate prophesies and patronizing accounts more seriously than its editors did.

II

The attitude of *Saturday Night* magazine was less consistent and therefore more interesting. On one occasion two editorials on Spain, each with different attitudes towards Fascism, appeared in the same issue:

> Canadians have no very strong opinion one way or the other about the present cleavage in Europe. They are as little likely to fight for the Fascist policy as on the same side with Russia, especially if the cause of Russian intervention were a revolutionary Spain in the midst of the excesses of a ghastly civil war.[6]

The second writer was less neutral:

> In the last two years we have seen an increased suspicion of the Fascist countries and decreased alarm about the progress of Communism. Even the French language press, while naturally unsympathetic to Russia, has little kindness for the Hitler regime . . . The policies of the British government in recent years have contributed materially to the increase of Germany's strength and prestige.[7]

One month later, on October 3, 1936, more editorials on Spain appeared together, this time closer in viewpoint. The first writer saw Canadians as almost equally divided between Popular Front supporters and those in favour of the Rebels, while others did not feel they had enough wisdom to justify interfering:

> The war in Spain is a horrible thing but it is a war in Spain, just as the preceding war was a war in Ethiopia, and undoubtedly a logical consequence of the past behavior of various Spanish factions. Canada has to accept a share of responsibility for the tragedy of the Ethiopian, after failing to make good on the guarantees given. After that humiliating experience it is not surprising that we have metaphorically withdrawn into ourselves, and are profoundly thankful that we at least never guaranteed the Spaniards any protection against their own government or their own rebels.[8]

The second editorial began, "The business of Canada is to preserve the completest possible detachment," and ended with the following statement:

> Canada will be a much better neighbour to the rest of the world and will pursue a much more intelligible and predictable course, if henceforth she governs her external policy by what looks to be best for her own interests, and not by any considerations drawn from an international moral code too lofty for application in an emergency.[9]

Perhaps the inspiration for these editorials was a report in the same issue of Mr. King's speech to the League of Nations, in which he told Europe to

HONEST, MISTER, THERE'S NOBODY HERE BUT US SPANIARDS

Saturday Night, Toronto, March 1939. National Library of Canada/NL-15928.

straighten her affairs out for herself, and to look for no help from Canada except a little advice.

Later in October, an article by a University of Toronto French-language professor described the Spanish revolution as "the height of barbarism, ferocity and stupidity," and the Loyalist forces as "intoxicated with wine, blood and the smell of gunpowder."[10] The November 14th issue referred to the visit to Montreal by the delegates of the Spanish government, commenting that it was odd how Socialists clamoured for liberty at the same time as they preached slavery to the state, and saying that their interference with liberty made Fascism almost inevitable.

These editorials in favour of Canadian non-intervention were countered by the ironic approach of Hugh Shoobridge. A sample of his work appeared at the time of the bombing of Bilbao and Guernica:

General Franco had a form printed in order to cope quickly and competently with each issue as it arose:-

"The National Spanish Government

Greatly Deeply Sincerely } regrets that owing to { Communist trickery Mistaken zeal Low visibility

an unfortunate error was made by the { Army Navy Air Force

resulting in damage to His Majesty's { Ship Subject Territory

The greatest care is always taken but still mistakes are liable to be made on proof of which our apologies can always be obtained. All protests should be accompanied by stamped addressed envelopes for reply."[11]

Welcome rally for Tim Buck held at Maple Leaf Gardens Stadium after his release from Kingston Penitentiary in November 1934. 17,000 attended, 8,000 were turned away. National Archives of Canada/PA-124370. Photo by E. Mackintosh.

As the war drew to a close, *Saturday Night*'s attitude began to change, as happened in other publications. An interesting editorial in January 1939 first regretted that the Loyalist cause was represented in Canada almost entirely by friends and members of the Mackenzie-Papineau Battalion who, while they had shown great courage and devotion to an ideal, were all convinced Communists. It continued:

> The identification of the Loyalist cause with the Mackenzie-Papineau Battalion seems to us to be merely adding to the already serious misunderstanding in Canada of the nature of the Spanish struggle. It is true that the Loyalists have been supported by Russia as the Franco government has been by Germany and Italy. But it is an extraordinary thing that Canadian public opinion should have passionately sympathised with Czechoslovakia under the same situation and be so generally cold to a Spanish government which received the same aid against the same enemies and now seems likely to receive the same treatment from France and Britain.[12]

A letter denied the claim that the Canadian volunteers were all Communists, naming members of the Mac-Paps who were Liberal, Conservative or, like S.H. Abramson, officials of a Zionist youth organization:

> If today there exists among sections in Canada a confused and indifferent attitude toward the Spanish Republic, this can be attributed largely to the open and surreptitious campaign of misrepresentation on the part of certain high ecclesiastical personages and the pro-Fascist and unfair editorial policy of a certain influential section of the Canadian Press, which persists in labelling the legal and democratically-elected Spanish government as "Red" and General Franco's motley crew of Moors, Italians and Germans as "Nationalists".[13]

C.C.F. CHIEF OPENS NATIONAL CONVENTION

Communist party hopes of forming a United Front, bringing into the C.C.F. organization a number of other organizations, were blasted by J. S. Woodsworth, M.P., leader of the C.C.F. group in parliament and chairman of the National Council, in his address yesterday which opened the National convention of the C.C.F. party. Mr. Woodsworth (LEFT) is shown talking over the situation with Graham Spry (RIGHT), of the provincial executive.

Toronto Star, August 4, 1936. Metropolitan Toronto Library Board photo.

An editorial in the same issue accepted that all the Mac-Paps were not Communists and admitted that, "whatever their economic beliefs, they went gladly into great danger for the sake of what they unquestionably believed to be in the best interests of humanity and justice."[14]

Saturday Night's final editorial on the war in Spain expressed

> relief that the mutual slaughter of Spaniards is ended, combined with the hope that General Franco will pursue justice rather than vengeance in dealing with the conquered. If the Franco Rebellion had not been preceded by so large a measure of Communist activity in Spain the sympathies of Canadians would have been much more definitely on the side of the late Government.[15]

It appears that the leading Canadian periodicals, like the newspapers that had defended the Right throughout the Spanish Civil War, were more willing to acknowledge the Loyalists and their cause after they were safely defeated.

III

When the CCF Party emerged, the Communist Party termed its members "social fascists," and tried to disrupt the movement. Although that attitude changed with the formation of the Popular Front, when the CCF became comrades on the left, the relationship between the two parties was never an easy one. Also, the fact that the Communist Party was eager to work with the CCF in the Loyalist cause did not increase its popularity. We read statements by the Spanish government that it would prefer help from France and Britain rather than Russia, but Russia was ready to help.

Many members of the CCF advocated support for the Loyalists, but were hampered by divisions in the party's thinking on foreign policy. Christian Pacifists like J.S. Woodsworth vied with those who believed that the League of Nations could be restored as an instrument of collective security, and with those who wished to establish an independent foreign policy for Canada. Some CCF party members hesitated to join Communist-controlled Popular Front organizations like the League Against War

and Fascism, even in such a good cause as support of Loyalist Spain, while men like Frank Scott, Graham Spry and Frank Underhill led the support of CCF members across Canada for the Loyalists. In the House of Commons, M.J. Coldwell, David Lewis, Angus MacInnis and Grant MacNeil defended the cause of the Spanish government to no avail.

By September 5, 1936, the *New Commonwealth,* the official organ of the CCF, had already referred to the war in Spain several times as one of class warfare, and on that date an editorial opposed Britain's non-intervention policy,

> which means intervention or weighing the scales in favor of fascism. The British Government fears war and it fears even more than war another Socialist or Communist government in Europe. This policy is scarcely justified by fear of war, for the one way to prevent Spain from becoming a cause of war was to sustain the Spanish democratic government. If that government loses Spain will become a vassal of Germany or Italy, and this will end the British Command of the Mediterranean.[16]

Later in September, a carefully worded lead story appeared on the front page:

> A national Committee to be known as the Spanish Hospital and Medical Aid Committee is being established to finance a field hospital unit as a gift from Canadian citizens to the Spanish Red Cross. Non-political in character, it will appeal for support on humanitarian and broad democratic and liberal grounds, and will represent a wide section of Canadian opinion, including church, academic and professional representatives as well as trade union, social and other organizations.[17]

The author, Graham Spry, editor of the paper, felt that action must be taken to unite the CCF in support of the Spanish government before the project was taken over completely by the Communists. Both Eugene Forsey and Graham Spry told me the concern was a legitimate one, because "the Communists worked full time on these committees and all the others could not."

Dr. Norman Bethune in front of the truck of the Canadian Blood Transfusion Service with inset photos of his helpers Hazen Sise, Henning Sorensen and Allen May, 1937. National Archives of Canada/PA-114782.

Mr. Spry had decided that the project of financing a hospital would appeal to all factions of the CCF, as well as to a wider section of the population, and he told me that he wrote the article with no one else's knowledge or support of any kind. Much to his surprise, Dr. Norman Bethune phoned from Montreal the following day, saying that he would like to join the organization and could leave for Spain at once!

This version of the story of Bethune's involvement, along with an editorial in *New Frontier* in December 1936, contradicts Tim Buck's claim in an article published in the *Marxist Quarterly* in 1966 that Dr. Bethune had taken the initiative and had approached the Communist Party in Quebec with the suggestion that it organize a blood transfusion unit in Spain.[18]

The figure of the "undisciplined, flamboyant and heroic"[19] Norman Bethune was responsible for much of the personal interest shown by Canadians during the first year of the war. In October, he left for Spain where he discovered there was great need for mobile blood transfusion units. The Committee to Aid Spanish Democracy took over the project of raising the money to purchase these units. Dr. Bethune was put in charge of the blood transfusion service for Madrid, assisted by Hazen Sise, a young Montreal architect whom he had met in London. Later he worked with refugees from Malaga who were bombed en route to Almeria. He also obtained help from the Spanish aid committee to set up children's villages for war orphans north of Barcelona.

In June 1937, he returned to Canada to bring the needs of Spain to the attention of Canada and the United States, and in an effort to have the embargo on arms lifted. In contrast to the Spanish delegates' reception, Dr. Bethune's arrival in Montreal was unmarred by opposition. Professor Scott believed Montreal officials regretted the poor publicity they had received from the previous incident. Under the headline, "8000 Pack Avenue to Greet Bethune and

Dr. Bethune helping women and children into his truck on the seventh day of the retreat from Malaga, 1937. National Archives of Canada/PA-124407.

Aid Loyalists," the Montreal *Gazette* reported:

> no trouble developed, police were on guard but not needed. . . . He [Bethune] drew the simile of Mr. Bennett calling in the Japanese and starting a march on Montreal after his defeat. Mr. King would be trying to defend Montreal with a handful of poor police and militia and might be asking the United States for help in buying arms. The United States would refuse the aid because of the fear of starting a war in Greenland. This is a perfect parallel of the Spanish situation.[20]

Carried shoulder-high through the crowds at the station, Bethune had asked Canadians to assume the care of 500 child refugees. Despite the philanthropic nature of this appeal, Mr. Spry spoke of having received donations from Dr. Banting and Sir Robert Falconer who requested that their names not be mentioned.

Dr. Bethune spoke to large crowds across Canada and showed a film, *Heart of Spain,* on the work of his blood transfusion units. When war broke out in China, he felt he was needed there and he left Canada for the last time. The *New Commonwealth's* stand on the Civil War was clear from the beginning and its part in originating Dr. Bethune's work the most interesting contribution it made to the Loyalist cause.

Dr. Bethune during his tour of Canada to raise   Archives of Canada/PA-116900.
money for medical aid to Spain, 1937. National

Float urging support for Dr. Bethune's unit in Spain – part of the May Day parade in Edmonton, Alberta, 1937. City of Edmonton Archives EA 160-1242.

IV

The *Federationist* was unlike any of the other publications I examined in its outlook and its attitude to the Spanish Civil War. It gave the impression of being a CCF organ superimposed on a labour paper, and research proved this to be the case. The *Federationist* had begun early in the 20th century as the voice of the B.C. Federation of Labour, around the same time as the founding of the Socialist Party in B.C. in 1901. According to Dorothy Steeves, the *Commonwealth,* begun in 1933 as the official CCF newspaper, expired in 1936 after it followed Mr. Connell, the ex-leader, into exile. So the *Federationist* came into being as a combination of the views of both papers, with the added complication that its staff was strongly against the idea of a united front of all leftist groups. The position of the CCF party in B.C. on this issue was similarly complex, with men whom Mr. Connell had called Marxists working to oust A.M. Stephen, head of the League against War and Fascism, from the party. While the *Federationist's* declared support for the Loyalists never wavered, its columns often reflected a tough and bitter attitude towards society.

The *Federationist* was not available for examination for the period covering the first six months of the Civil War, and, in the first issue examined, we read that "thirteen men, a number of them well known in the labour movement here, left Vancouver late last week on the first leg of an extended trip to Spain where they will aid the Loyalist forces."[21]

On March 25, 1937, Dr. Telford, head of the CCF in British Columbia, defended Mr. Stephen's suspension from the party, "which is, or should be, the real United Front for Canada." Angus MacInnis reported that Communists had been abusing members of the CCF who resisted joining the United Front, among them the editor of the *Federationist,* Don Smith, who was accused of being a Trotskyist. Smith retorted, "The *Federationist* has supported consistently the fight of the Spanish people, and will continue to do so, when accused of not doing this, or of not supporting the Popular Front or the united front of all progressive groups in B.C."[22] Letters poured in from branches of the party all over the province, vehement in support or condemnation of the United Front, but taking a definite position, something the party in B.C. failed to do at this time.

News reports on the war in Spain were all optimistic, with many photographs. The ideological

Aid to Spain meeting in Vernon, British Columbia, July 1937. Glenbow Archives, Calgary, Alberta NA-3634-17.

picture is not too clear, for, below articles on President Luis Companys of Catalonia, whose independent government was hated by the Communists, there is an interview with a British Columbia woman who had just returned from a trip to Russia, where she had "seen in people's eyes, not contentment or submission but surety and happiness."[23] She found conditions "in a kaleidoscopic state," rather a mild term to describe the period of the Moscow trials.

In June 1937, it was announced that Dr. Bethune would speak in Vancouver, sponsored by the Spanish aid committee of the League against War and Fascism. In July, the CCF took a stand against supporting the League or uniting with the Communists, but it did support Bethune's appearance. The League office on West Hastings was also the headquarters for a Girls' Volunteer Brigade to aid Spain. The *Federationist* reported on this at some length, the only time I encountered mention of such an organization. It had been created to raise money for a home for Spanish orphans, and in two weeks six girls had raised $150, a large amount in those days:

To become a member, a girl raises $2, $5 more entitles her to a red cadet cap, and $10 more a red

three-cornered scarf. Another $15 gives her a Mac-Pap badge. Three girls have already done this and were presented with their badges Saturday night by Dr. Bethune.[24]

Dr. Bethune told of his work, which included treating Italian and German prisoners, and showed the film, *Heart of Spain*. The fact that he spoke to the Chamber of Commerce in Victoria indicates that acceptance of his work on the west coast was not just among radicals.

In September 1937, the *Federationist* printed the official policy the CCF party had adopted on Spain at its convention: that the Non-Intervention Pact should be ended and the legitimate government of Spain allowed to purchase military supplies in the markets of the world, with that privilege denied to the Rebel forces, and that the League of Nations take immediate action to name Italy and Germany aggressors against the government of Spain.

According to the *Federationist,* political feelings ran very high in British Columbia at this time. The issue of January 6, 1938 reported that copies of the paper had been destroyed at Gray Creek, and that a man had lost his job in the ensuing quarrel. The same issue carried a report of a speech by Leo

Sweeney, head of a cooperage firm in Vancouver, who felt that a little Nazism would be a good thing for the Canadian government. He later modified this statement when asked to speak to the Trades and Labour Council on the subject. More than any newspaper, the *Federationist* reflected the atmosphere of deprivation and cynicism that existed in the 1930s: a bitter "social column" parodied the items usually found in that section of a newspaper, and the police were always in the wrong, in print or cartoon. Russian films were reviewed in detail and seemed to have a high rate of frequency in Vancouver. Several articles expressed differing views on the Moscow trials.

The editorials were usually on labour issues, but the many news reports and comments on Spain continued to hope for a Loyalist victory. Several letters were published from John Offer of the Mac-Paps, who was impressed by the courage of the Spanish people. He wrote, "I have met a lot of the Vancouver fellows I used to know, and I'm surprised at the large number of CCF members here."[25] In a later letter, he stated that it was the duty of the people of Canada to support the Spanish people in striking a blow at Fascism, for, "in spite of mistakes and certain bad aspects of organization, the Spanish government commands the unstinted support of a majority of the Spanish people."[26]

There were 10,000 people in the Vancouver parade on May Day, 1938, with the press secretary of the Union General del Trabajadores (UGT) there from Madrid to speak at a public meeting on the same day. On June 16th, the *Federationist* requested contributions for the Spanish Orphans' Home, and announced the Girls' Brigade was sponsoring a "Night in Old Madrid" concert for the same cause. Requests also appeared from time to time for soap, cigarettes, etc. for the Mac-Paps, and any speeches made by the CCF members of Parliament about the war in Spain were reprinted.

On February 9, 1939, one of the few Canadian cartoons on the Civil War showed Chamberlain handing over a bleeding and heart-shaped Spain to Mussolini for Valentine's Day. The paper's final editorial on the war, "In Spain Today," was an exceptionally strong one:

> From the tidings that come from Spain these days the sand is running short in the hour glass of liberty. Bleeding, betrayed, Loyalist Spain seems near its end. Although the Loyalists would fight on, Franco and his allies have now all but battered their way to power.
>
> The part the democracies have played in the tragedy that is Spain is too well known, too blackly marked to need recapitulation here. Their refusal to deal with a people's government has made Britain and France accomplices to the crime, as guilty of the murder of the innocents as Mussolini.
>
> Fascism is preferable to socialism as far as capitalist governments are concerned. Sliding toward its economic doom, capitalism is clutching for a hold upon the cliffs of time. And with its hideous and barbaric reversions, fascism offers that hold.
>
> Franco, suggests the News-Herald, is perhaps not such a bad fellow. When he has curbed the "rebels" he will clean out the foreign influences.
>
> Truly fascism knows no international boundaries – pro-fascist newspapers help us learn that it begins at home.

There is also a news item reporting that 50 members of the Mac-Paps, who fought gallantly for a just cause in Spain, would be arriving the following Friday: "While government and military circles here disdain to welcome the Mac-Paps the working people will welcome them, with a delegation from the Trades and Labour Council and the C.C.F. bandsmen."[27] This final note exemplifies the attitude of the *Federationist,* which portrayed the Loyalist cause as the embodiment of the cause of the common worker and the underdog throughout the war.

WON'T YOU BE MY VALENTINE?

The Federationist, Vancouver, February 9, 1939.
National Library of Canada/NL-15851.

—Pegi Nicol

MERRY CHRISTMAS

December, 1936.

Canadian Forum, Toronto, December 1936. National Library of Canada/NL-15921.

V

The *Canadian Forum* was founded in 1920 as an independent journal of opinion to discuss new developments in the arts and in public affairs. A popular magazine for intellectuals, its image was that of·a moderate left, university group centered in Toronto. Under the editorship of Graham Spry in 1935, the *Forum* expanded its interest to French Canada and the visual arts. Mr. Spry sold the *Forum* to the League for Social Reconstruction in the summer of 1936.

In September 1936, the *Forum,* like most pro-Loyalist publications, was very definite in its stand, both on the question of Spain and ideologically:

The armed uprising engineered by Spanish Army officers against a freely elected government is so flagrantly illegal that even the right wing press in other countries has had no other choice than to call them rebels . . . They [Spain's troubles] reveal very clearly how the class struggle converts domestic into international politics, every country in Europe is swayed by the Spanish Civil War, according to its political beliefs.[28]

The *Forum* found it difficult to decide which was more nauseating, the cowardice and hypocrisy of Spain's democratic neighbours, or the mutual slaughter of the Spaniards themselves:

The government is denied the right to purchase arms, and we suspect, food and medical supplies from abroad. Fascist powers have established embassies with the rebels and furnished them with credits. The embargo imposed on the Civil War by the rest of Europe is the worst sort of hypocrisy, for, by being applied to Spain itself, the supposed seat of conflict, it automatically cuts off Madrid while allowing every sort of weapon to pass through Lisbon and Morocco, the real bases of the rebellion.[29]

The November issue presented statistics that backed up that statement: in September 1935, Canadian exports to Morocco amounted to $1,924 worth of goods; by September 1936, the value of such exports had risen to $296,752. These figures were confirmed in *Hansard* for February 15, 1937, by which time it was known that exports to Morocco for the last four months of 1935 were worth $45,000 compared to those for the same period in 1936 at approximately $1,775,000. In Canada, as in Europe, neutrality was preached but not practised.

Another strong editorial appeared in September 1937:

Democrats all over the world now hold their noses at the very mention of non-intervention in Spain. Mr. King chooses this moment to apply to Spain his new Foreign Enlistment Act, and an even newer measure to control the arms traffic. A Canadian "Liberal" Government has placed on the same footing a legally constituted democratic government with which it is supposed to be on friendly diplomatic relations and the rebels against that government.[30]

From then on, the only optimistic editorial on the war was one expressing the conviction that the tide had turned at Teruel.

There was less material concerning the Civil War in the *Forum* than I had expected, and more emphasis on the Civil Liberties Union and its stand in Quebec. However, the *Forum's* coverage of the arts was indicative of the strong influence of the war on artists in the Thirties. A series of articles on artists included Charles Comfort and Paraskeva Clark, both of whom wrote and painted in support of the Loyalist cause. The work of Montreal artists of European extraction like Louis Muhlstock and Alexander Bercowitz gave similar support. Many poems, such as Louis MacKay's "Battle Hymn for the Spanish Rebels" and Norman Bethune's "Red Moon" were printed here. Little fiction appeared in the *Forum,* none of it about the Spanish Civil War.

The letters to the editor in the *Forum* give an indication of how difficult it was to unify Loyalist support in Canada. In December 1937, "a journalist and leader of Youth Organizations in Montreal" wrote from Spain about the success of the Loyalist campaign and the popularity of the International Brigade in supporting the People's Front for a free Republican Spain. In April 1938, Henry Scott Beattie, also a volunteer, stated that the International Brigade was unpopular with the average man and that he broke with the Communist Party when

January, 1937

Canadian Forum, Toronto, January 1937. National Library of Canada/NL-15923.

he found out the Communist International was supporting the Brigade's policy. He asserted that the Communist Party supported Spanish capitalism, that the masses hated the Popular Front, and that it was the Anarchists and Poumites who stopped Franco. In the next issue, Larry K. Ryan attacked Beattie with that supreme epithet, "Trotskyite," and accused him of making his story up on his return to Canada after a very brief stay in the front lines. One can see why citizens who might have been sympathetic towards the Spanish government hesitated to align themselves with such doctrinaire allies.

As part of its interest in civil rights, the *Forum* supported the case of the Spanish government delegates in several articles, and reported the action of the Civil Liberties Union in preventing Mayor Raynault of Montreal and Archbishop Gauthier from presiding at a meeting addressed by a Spanish Rebel, Jose Pedroso, in Plateau Hall in March 1938.

Although the *Forum* supported Loyalist Spain throughout the war, one might say it gave strong intellectual and rational support, compared to the political and emotional dedication to the cause demonstrated by *New Frontier*.

VI

New Frontier's first issue declared two-fold aims: to acquaint the Canadian public with the work of those writers and artists who expressed a positive reaction to social problems; and to serve as an open forum for all shades of progressive opinion.

Though many of the contributors to *New Frontier* also wrote for the *Forum*, *New Frontier*'s policy was much more radical, and its editorial board was comprised of many Party members and fellow-travellers. Nowhere else did I discover such complete absorption in the Loyalist cause. *New Frontier* survived for only 18 months, from April 1936 to October 1937, but every issue contained material on Spain: poems, stories, news items, articles, translations. In fact, one entire issue was devoted to the subject of the Spanish Civil War.

As early as June 1936, *New Frontier* was advocating an anti-capitalist United Front for Canada following the victory of Blum and his United Front in the June elections in France. By September, the Communist Party line was very obvious:

The insurgents continue to fight like the cornered rats they are. With little support among the people, their main strength lies in the army command, the mercenary troops of the Foreign Legion and peasants from the most backward provinces. . . . Despite the vacillations of the liberals and many leaders of the Socialist Party, in the face of a campaign of sabotage organised by Anarchist and Syndicalist leaders, the People's Front has proven itself the only force capable of fighting off the fascist reaction and clearing the way for the forces of progress. For Canadians the lesson of Spain is clear, the only hope for democracy, peace and progress in this country is a People's Front, including all sections of the working and middle class.[31]

New Frontier compared the leadership of the Soviet Union in defending peace and democracy to the position taken by Prime Minister King: "The Soviet position is in sharp contrast to the repudiation of collective security and the tacit support of fascist aggression voiced before the League by Premier King."[32]

The writer read with appreciation an article by Leonard Walsh in the issue of October 1936, entitled "Red Atrocities, Read All about Them," for all the examples it gave of prejudiced reporting occurred in the newspapers which I have already described in Chapter 3.

The December 1936 issue was devoted almost entirely to articles and opinions on the Spanish crisis. Father Sarasola defended the Loyalist government, and one article dealt with the delegates' visit and the increasingly fascist atmosphere of Quebec. Another focussed on three great Spanish women, Dolores Ibarruri, known as "La Pasionaria," and two socialist deputies, Maria Sierra and Margarita Nelkin.

The most relevant part of this issue is a section entitled, "Where I stand on Spain," with contributions by people from many walks of life, including the Trades and Labour Congress of Canada. Rabbi Maurice Eisendrath remarked that, if the legitimate government of Spain were defeated through cowardice and dissembling, the lights would go out in Europe one by one. The Reverend Salem Bland of the United Church called Rebel sympathizers Fascists at heart, and stated that if Spain falls, it will fall not only through the efforts of

New Frontier, January 1937, Metropolitan Toronto
Library Board photo.

500 Canadians in Spain
Fighting for Democracy!

The Friends of the Mackenzie-Papineau Battalion has been organized to provide them with books (not necessarily new) cigarettes, tobacco, soap, etc. Please send donations to

Friends of the Mackenzie-Papineau Battalion
Peace Centre   929 Bay Street   Toronto

New Frontier, July-August 1937, Metropolitan Toronto Library Board photo.

its foes, but also through the timidity of its friends. Artist Charles Comfort made an impassioned plea for the Loyalists, while to novelist Morley Callaghan supporters of the Rebels valued property rights over human rights. Poet E.J. Pratt gave four popular reasons for supporting the Loyalists and for his fifth and last, "A hundred other unprintable reasons." One exception was B.K. Sandwell, editor of *Saturday Night,* who did not see much to choose between the sides, saying he felt about the Civil War as he would "about a conflict between two rival members of the Hapsburg family in Austria before the Great War."[33]

In January 1937, *New Frontier* attributed the reduced votes for the CCF in Toronto, not to lack of organization as it claimed, but to its confused policy and its opposition to the United Front, out of "petty spitefulness, which has made *New Commonwealth* the instrument of a clique of right wing leaders."[34] The *Canadian Forum* was also attacked, in March, for advertising a "scurrilous pamphlet" on the Moscow trials.

Articles by Ted Allan, entitled "Blood for Spanish Democracy" and "Bombardment at Albacete," as well as an interview with Ernest Hemingway, were more interesting. Allan was the Madrid correspondent for the *Clarion* and also a stringer for A.P. He and Jean Watts, another *Clarion* reporter, were involved in preparing *Spanish Earth,* a film on the Canadian blood transfusion service with dialogue written by Hemingway and direction by Joris Ivens. Allan and Watts both broadcast on short wave from Madrid, requesting contributions in order to supply 5,000 quarts of milk to Spanish babies. Jean Watts was also a frequent contributor to *New Frontier* of such varied material as a story on Spain and a report on André Malraux's appearances in Montreal and Toronto to raise money for hospital supplies.

Art work by Fritz Brandtner and Louis Muhlstock, poetry by Dorothy Livesay and A.M. Stephen, and translations of Spanish poems by W.E. Collins also appeared in the magazine.

The May 1937 issue contained an interesting article about the French-language publication *L'Unité,* 30,000 copies of which were being distributed weekly to 1,218 parishes in Quebec. Advertisements signed by M.R. Beaudoin, treasurer of "Aide aux Catholiques d'Espagne," solicited money for war materials "to help General Franco win his Moorish-Italian-German war against Spanish Democracy," in the words of *New Frontier.* It further commented that, while the paper was not breaking the law, "contributing and presumably forwarding money for war materials was a blatant defiance of the attitude which Canada has taken in its parliament to the struggle in Spain."[35]

The final issue of *New Frontier* appeared in October 1937 and contained the information that Canadian manufacturers had sold Franco $100,000 worth of planes and parts sent by way of Portugal between April and June 1937. The only shipment to the Loyalists during that period was $3,500 worth of condensed milk. At that time, the magazine was appealing for financial support, not surprising when a one-year subscription cost one dollar.

All the material on Spain in *New Frontier* is well written and convincing, perhaps because the magazine purported to be fully engaged in the contemporary political scene. I found more gusto and conviction in its pages than in those of the *Forum,* cuttingly described by *New Frontier* as "a rather genteel sprig clipped from the suburban hedge of British Fabianism."[36]

The pro-Loyalist publications described in this chapter presented a rational defence of the legal government of Spain, which should have been backed by the League of Nations. To find the emotional appeal of the Loyalist cause, one must turn to the literature of the period.

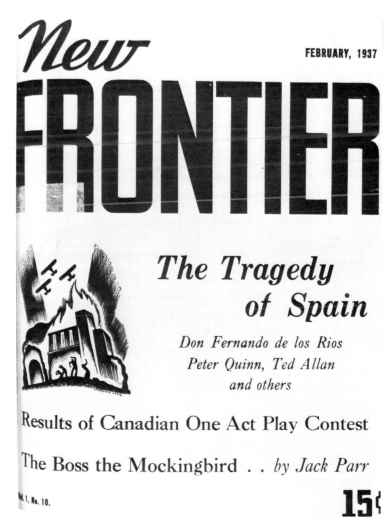

Cover of *New Frontier,* February 1937, Metropolitan Toronto Library Board photo.

CHAPTER 5

"The Crystal Spirit"

Your name and your deeds were forgotten
Before your bones were dry,
And the lie that slew you is buried
Under a deeper lie.

But the thing that I saw in your face
No power can disinherit;
No bomb that ever burst
Shatters the crystal spirit.
　　– "Looking Back on the Spanish War,"
　　　　　　　　　　　George Orwell

In his book on the Spanish Civil War, Hugh Thomas refers to a poll taken of British writers: only 5 supported the Nationalists, 16 were neutral and 100 were committed, usually in passionate terms, to Republican Spain. In Canada, I could find no evidence of literary support for the Nationalists.

The jingoistic spirit of the first years of this century changed in the 1920s, when concern with one's country became joined to an optimistic desire to see and remedy its faults. The coming of industrial urban society and the dark years of the 1930s helped turn what had been perceived as a proletarian minority into a major force as a class, and this was reflected in a literary and cultural movement, as many artists and writers empathized with the proletariat and the need to support the Spanish government. Poets were especially active in defending the Loyalist cause, and many poems appeared in the *Canadian Forum* and *New Frontier*. According to Earle Birney's review of *Poems for Spain*, edited by Stephen Spender, that appeared in the *Forum* in

April of 1939, the ideological approach was not always in the best interests of art:

Many are sheer cries of pain, physical as well as spiritual; others are moving laments for Spain ravaged, for poets dead, for all the dead; there is a section of satiric execration upon the betrayal of the "democratic" powers . . . However, a careful editing was done in the interests of the prestige of the Third International . . . [1]

As a result, Birney criticized the collection for "a conspicuous absence in the translations from the Spanish of any of the marching and fighting songs of the revolutionary anarchists or the P.O.U.M." Evidently in both England and Canada poetry was but another aspect of the struggle among the factions of the Left.

Canadian verse written on the war ranged widely, from translations from the Spanish, to short, satiric doggerel and lyrics, to long, emotional narrative poems. Satire was a popular vehicle in the 1930s. Louis MacKay wrote an amusing poem about the various regions of Spain, containing the following verse:

Consider first the pious Basque,
It seemed a little thing to ask,
Peaceful permission to recline
Beneath his fig-tree and his vine
(Also above his iron mine)
Electing presidents and such
And bothering nobody much.[2]

The emotional poems were laments for the dead, or for personal loss. Dorothy Livesay's "Spain," first published in *New Frontier* in June 1937, is a universal cry for expiation and remembrance of the dead. A classic war poem, it merits repeating here:

When the bare branch responds to leaf and light,
Remember them! It is for this they fight.
It is for hills uncoiling and the green thrust
Of spring, that they lie choked with battle dust.

You who hold beauty at your finger tips
Hold it, because the splintering gunshot rips
Between your comrades' eyes: hold it, across
Their bodies' barricade of blood and loss.

You who live quietly in sunlit space
Reading the *Herald* after morning grace,
Can count peace dear, when it has driven
Your sons to struggle for this grim new heaven.[3]

A more concentrated appeal to humanity was made in the short poem "Salutes," by Lionel Reid, in the August 1938 issue of the *Forum:*

Rome ..... over a reviewing stand
the stout dictator's empty hand.
Madrid ..... the tightly folded fist
Of a dead baby Loyalist.[4]

One example of poetry of personal loss placed in the context of renewed dedication to the cause of fraternity and democracy, "To L-- B--" appeared in the September *Forum.* The first part of the poem describes the beauties of nature so loved by this man, a volunteer from British Columbia, and continues:

All these his life
He bartered these for death.
The brief adventure in a distant Spain –
His far horizon.
The mute and darkened blue of eyes that stared
Unseeing at a hazy August sun,
Blood-red, the symbol of his destiny –
His tragic poem.
The bright ideal followed to the end,
The brave and pulsing hour with his brothers,
The eloquence of dedicated youth
Shaming the mumbling mouths that try to glow
With breath rhetorical and second hand

The dying embers of democracy –
This the soul-power of him.[5]

Few of the emotional poems failed to include the symbolic word "red," significant of the intensity of commitment to the Loyalists and their only defenders, Russia. It is worth noting that the Canadian tradition of poetry based on observation of a familiar landscape was of little value in Spain; poetry for the cause emphasized struggle and dedication, especially in an unfamiliar environment.

The *Forum* printed one of the most successful poems of the period, "Dust Patterns after the Revolution," by David Andrade, at the war's end:

Safe now with friends tonight, a thousand miles
    away,
We turn off the radio to listen to the wind,
And I see again the barricades thrown up
Against the guns, the splintering bullets, the
    whirling dust,
I hear again the red flag snapping over me,
Nailed to a broom-handle stuck in a barrel,
And I am deafened with the rattle of home-made
    rifles
And the heavy booming of guns at the end of the
    street.
These are the brave ones,
The factory hands, the clerks, the pick-and-shovel
    men
Fighting their unequal battle against the charging
    white cavalry
That breaks over them like a wave, out-rhymes,
    out-harmonizes,
Better weaponed, better equipped, backed by a
    uniform tradition.[6]

Andrade's poem also shows the strong identification of the need for revolution in art with the need for social revolution.

During this period, the distinguished Canadian poet A.M. Klein contributed many poems of social protest such as "Barricade Smith" and "Of Daumiers A Portfolio," to both the *Forum* and *New Frontier.* The most interesting of a trio he wrote on the Spanish Civil War was "Sonnet without Music," with its experimental, metaphorical approach:

Upon the piazza, haemophilic dons
delicately lift their sherry in the sun.

Dorothy Livesay, poet and political activist. Photo by Susan Gage, 1988.

And Still We Dream

And still we dream, coiled in a mountain crevice
And still we let the sun
Shift on flesh and bone his subtle fingers
Before his day is run.

Comrade, the thrush will never give us warning
His singing will not cease—
The bees will hum all down the darkest morning
Inveigling us to peace

The mountains, yearning forward into silence
Have done with shaking; and the stir
Of centuries is only a brief wrinkle
Where the thunders were.

But we, who like to lie here hushed, immobile,
Whistling a low bird note
Can have no rest from clash of arms behind us
And thunder at the throat:

Here, though we dream like lizards on a rock-ledge
Suckling the sun's breast—
Manhood and growth are on us; rise up, Comrade,
It is death to rest.

Man Asleep

Though hunched in grass as mountain rocks take root
Hunched over towns, their contours blocked and blurred
Receding at the march of evening, mute—

Though unresisting while the summer's hand
Smooths out your brow, relaxes the stiff bone
And cools the blood—somewhere the guns command.

There, dreaming one, your brothers raise the dust
Over Madrid, gird the impassive hills,
Cast off mandragora with lightning thrust;

There, sleeper, do the men like clouds oppress:
Stiffer than yours, their bones, their feet
Footsore with battle, not with homelessness.

See, the world's home they build in Spain—
The fireside stone you never had, the arms
You snatched at, but could not maintain.

Now hunched in sleep, you dream the battle's done:
But still your bones shall spring to life like steel
Clamp down on victory, behold the sun!

DOROTHY LIVESAY.

New Frontier, October 1936, Metropolitan Toronto Library Board photo.

Having recovered confiscated land
and his expropriated smile redeemed,
the magnate, too has doff'd his socialized face,
He beams a jocund aftermath to bombs.

Alas, the priest – alas for so much bloodshed! –
cups plumpish hand to catch uncatechized belch.

The iron heel grows rusty in the nape
of peasant feeding with the earthworm – but
beware Aristocrat, Don Pelph, beware!
The peon soon will stir, will rise, will stand,
breathe Hunger's foetid breath, lift arm, clench
    fist,
and heil you to the fascist realm of Death.[7]

It has been said that much of the poetry of this period has too little aesthetic value and too much ideological involvement, but it pushed at the barriers of tradition and helped create a wider range of freedom of subject matter. To quote F.W. Watt, "the conservative culture of nation-building met in full dialectical play the art and politics of protest and rebellion and each was transformed by the collision."[8] This new approach humanized and simplified the art of many poets, and out of it developed the poets of the 1940s, including Patrick Anderson, Louis Dudek, Irving Layton, P.K. Page and Earle Birney.

Two Canadian novels set in the period of the Spanish Civil War offer an interesting comparison. *This Time a Better Earth* by Ted Allan was published in 1939, while *The Watch That Ends the Night* by Hugh MacLennan was published much later.

Ted Allan, the *Clarion* reporter, was in Spain in 1936 and 1937. He was only 23 when his novel, described on the jacket as "a universal story of youth and its belief in an ideal," was published. It tells the story of Bob Curtis, a young Canadian writer and Communist in the International Brigade. Although overloaded with symbolism and rather derivatory, its naive and youthful idealism is quite moving.

Through Bob Curtis, we are introduced to five of his friends, who are all prototypes: Alan Linton, an actor from an old New England family; Milton Schwartz of Brooklyn; Lucien Poirier, a French Canadian; Harry Sills, an Alberta coal miner; and Doug Rollins, a black stockyard worker from Chicago. They meet when entering Spain, and their first stopping place, a fort in Catalonia, is the scene of a meeting where the Commandant welcomes them on behalf of the International Brigade, "where no politics exist." Each sings a song of his country and at the end of the meeting all join in singing the *Internationale*, a stirring moment.

We find a good deal of emphasis on Communist beliefs, such as the importance of the political commissar in the army, and of good organization against the POUM, who have tried to stab the Popular Front in the back.

The dialogue is reminiscent of Hemingway, as is the part of the story that concerns Lisa, the blonde German photographer who had left her family to live in Paris and then in Spain. Curtis remains in Madrid to make radio broadcasts to America, while his friends go to the front, one to meet his death and another to face permanent blindness. The bombardment of Madrid is described with horror and revulsion, but near the front, outside the city, the scene is pastoral and lovely, even the small hill dotted with olive trees and named "Suicide Hill."

When Bob and Lisa reach the scene of the fighting in order to take photographs, she is fatally injured by a tank while riding on the running board of a car, and both are hit in an air attack immediately afterwards. This incident and a doctor's statement that in the next World War more people would be insane from air bombardment than soldiers killed, epitomize the fear of a mechanized, technological society so evident in the literature of the 1930s.

None of the volunteers regret coming, whatever has befallen them. Doug Rollins' statement, "We're fightin' for a new kind of world where there's no hate, no fighting, just peace and quiet,"[9] could only have been written during a war, by a young idealistic author.

Peter Wyden's *The Passionate War* reveals that Allan's story of Lisa's death is based on an actual experience. Wyden records the death of Gerda Taro, a Jewish refugee from Germany, hit by a tank at Brunete. Gerda lived with Robert Capa who taught her photography. She had obtained permission to go to the front to take pictures of the action and invited Allan to go with her. The army began to retreat and they were urged to leave. According to Wyden, Allan was terrified but Gerda refused to go. When her roll of film was finished, she jumped on the running board of a car and was hit by a swerving tank. She died in hospital the next day.

Author Ted Allan who reported from Madrid during
the Civil War. Photo by Sam Shaw (1985).

At the beginning of *The Watch That Ends The Night*, George Stewart, also a radio broadcaster, describes the 1930s many years later:

Was there ever a time when so many people tried so pathetically to feel responsible for all mankind? Was there ever a generation which yearned to belong, so unsuccessfully, to something larger than themselves?[10]

By the time MacLennan's book was published in 1958, the hope and illusions are gone, for to have gone to Spain was "to be ruined forever. That was the one move a man could make in those days that was never forgiven after."[11] (The consequences of youthful idealism is also the theme of *Down the Long Table* by Earle Birney, whose descriptions of involvement with left-wing university groups in the 1930s are as realistic and vivid as Hugh MacLennan's of Communist meetings held in Montreal at the same time.)

The central figure in *The Watch That Ends the Night* is Dr. Jerome Martell, a dynamic, tempestuous figure based on Bethune. As his involvement with the Spanish war and the Communists grows, he speaks of his tragic childhood and defends his hatred of Fascism as "the organization of every murderous impulse in the human body. The old countries which gave us our civilization are tired of being civilized. But people like me, people born on the fringes, we really care."[12] Jerome returns from Spain disillusioned with Russia, but goes back after raising money for his surgical unit. Word has it that he is dead, but he reappears 12 years later when "nobody asked the big questions any more," as opposed to the Thirties when "no man was an island entire of itself."[13]

The most consistent theme in all the literature about Loyalist Spain is a feeling of responsibility for someone else, whether on humanitarian or ideological grounds. The depth of feeling about the 1930s and the Spanish Civil War expressed by the characters in MacLennan's book was typical of those who looked back on the period many years later.

Whatever their involvement in the Loyalist cause, writers of a later period never denied its emotional appeal. That men from many lands should meet as brothers to fight against inequality was a cause to appeal to the liberal and imaginative mind rather than to the conservative elements of society.

Gerald Brenan has written, "It is the nature of revolutions to throw up moments when all the more brilliant dreams of the human race seem about to be realized."[14] This feeling of dedication and hope for a better future is found in all the literature on the Spanish Civil War and the regret that the better world was not attained lingers long after.

Soldiers of the Mackenzie-Papineau Battalion in a trench in Spain, 1937 or 1938. National Archives of Canada/C-67469.

New Frontier, December 1936, Metropolitan Toronto Library Board photo.

CHAPTER 6

Vox Populi

One might expect that an examination of *Hansard* would imply turning from fiction to fact, but on the subject of the Spanish Civil War, *Hansard* resembled a mystery story more than anything else. Since most changes in government policy concerning the Spanish Civil War were acccomplished by means of Orders-in-Council, we only learn what happened through the references made to them in the House of Commons.

Not until May 1938 did Prime Minister Mackenzie King speak on the Spanish Civil War, although the CCF raised the issue several times prior to that. On January 19, 1937, Mr. O.B. Elliot asked Mr. King, "Is it the intention of the government to support the British policy of banning the recruiting of Canadian volunteers for the civil war in Spain?" Mr. King replied "that the control of enlistment in Canada for military service has been under examination. Canada is not on the non-intervention committee. The question, however, will continue to be given consideration."[1] On January 29th, Mr. Coldwell was told in reply to a question that the government intended to introduce legislation on the subject of foreign service now that Great Britain had given its opinion on the subject.

On February 18th, the Hon. Earnest Lapointe, Minister of Justice, introduced Bill 23 respecting foreign enlistment. Parliament gave its assent on April 10th, and on July 31st the act was applied to the Spanish Civil War.

Two sections of the act were relevant to Loyalist volunteers from Canada. Section 3 forbade enlistment in the armed forces of any foreign state at war with a friendly state. However, no mention was made of enlistment in insurgent armies within friendly states, so, theoretically, a Canadian volunteer could fight for the Nationalists against Loyalist Spain. Moreover, Section 19 gave discretionary powers of application of the act to the government.

At the start of the debate, Mr. Woodsworth stated that he personally was in favour of neutrality, but it must be a thorough-going neutrality. A long debate revolved around his question, "Why should not prohibitions which are directed against assistance to states at war with friendly states also apply against assistance to rebels against a friendly state?"[2] Such a prohibition had been omitted from the bill, and the CCF feared the discretionary powers of the government. Justice Minister Lapointe assured the House that in Britain the act applied to both sides of the conflict, and "if the conflict is not of such a kind that the provisions of the act apply to it, there would be no intervention on one side or the other."[3] To this Mr. Douglas retorted that the act should not be left to the government to apply at its discretion, but should be applied from the beginning of the conflict. When Mr. MacNeil questioned the proposed cancellation of passports for Spain as interfering with civil liberties, Mr. Lapointe replied, "We do not want our people to go abroad to fight in these conflicts, and one of the best ways to prevent them is through the control of passports. *Salus populi suprema lex:* 'The state does not desire to be involved in difficulties.' "[4] This was a rather strange translation from the Latin, "the health of the people is the supreme law."

Volunteers aboard the *S.S. President Roosevelt* on their way to Spain in 1937. National Archives of Canada/C-67465.

On March 30th, Mr. Lapointe mentioned the many letters and cables he had received denouncing the Foreign Enlistment Act. Since some bore the same wording, he suggested that they were obviously the result of a propaganda campaign to discredit and prevent the passage of the act – a correct assumption on his part.

Debate on the bill closed with questions on Section 2(b), which excluded from the definition of "armed forces" medical and other services engaged in humanitarian work, if they were under control of the Canadian Red Cross or another recognized Canadian humanitarian society. Bethune's blood transfusion unit was not mentioned, but such recently established schemes would obviously be tightly controlled from then on. The bill finally passed after the CCF forced the government to spend the entire afternoon session defending it.

Throughout passage of the bill through the House, volunteers were leaving Canada for the war in Spain and needed passports. Many of the B.C.

volunteers had served in the relief camps and knew each other. Dr. Lyle Telford, a CCF leader in Vancouver, vouched for the character of these men on their way "to the Paris Exposition." After the government moved to restrict passports on August 10, 1937, Canadian volunteers left with passports stamped "Not Valid for Spain." By that time, 500 volunteers were already in Spain, and the 700 who went after the application of the act ceased to exist in the eyes of the Canadian government.

On March 17, 1938, Mr. MacInnis asked that the embargo on exports to Spain imposed the previous year be removed, as it was now established that Germany and Italy were sending troops and supplies to fight against the legitimate government. Prime Minister King replied that the embargo applied only to arms and munitions similar to action taken by the non-intervention committee. He said, "we would wish at all cost to avoid making the present appalling situation on the two continents mentioned [Europe and Asia] more embarrassing for the coun-

CCF Members of Parliament in 1937. Left to right: T.C. Douglas, Angus MacInnis, A.A. Heaps, Party Leader J.S. Woodsworth, M.J. Coldwell, Grace MacInnis, Grant MacNeil. Photograph (c) 1937, Yousuf Karsh. Manitoba Archives/Events 246.

tries faced with it."[5]

On May 24th, Mr. King made a lengthy statement on foreign policy; in fact, his speech covers 15 pages in *Hansard*. He described the formation of the non-intervention committee and alluded to its failure to prevent extensive participation by outside states:

Its critics in England and France contend that it was unfair to put an unrecognised insurgent force on a par with a recognised government, and that a serious danger exists of a threat to British and French communications in the Mediterranean. Its sponsors contend that it has lessened the amount of such intervention, that it has prevented an open break which would have led inevitably to a general European war.[6]

Nevertheless he explained that, in order to localize the conflict and prevent Canada from being drawn into it, Orders-in-Council were passed in July 1937 to prohibit exports of munitions and to apply the Foreign Enlistment Act to the Spanish conflict. The control of exports was done through an amendment to the Customs Act; the Foreign Enlistment Act now applied to the Civil War, as an organized recruiting scheme was under way.

Two days later, Mr. MacInnis, in a long and impassioned speech, called the non-intervention committee the world's greatest farce, and the policy of its member nations towards Spain immoral. He pointed out the government of Canada had had a year to see what was happening in Spain, but had placed its embargo on sending goods to the legal government while continuing to ship supplies to Germany and Italy from which they could make munitions. He said that Spain, as a member of the

Prime Minister W.L. Mackenzie King receiving a Nazi salute in Berlin, Germany, 1937. National Archives of Canada/PA-119013.

League of Nations, should have received help and that the policy of the democratic countries could only harm democracy and lead to Communism or Fascism in Spain. He closed by asking that the embargo be rescinded, and was followed by Mr. Tommy Church, a Progressive Conservative, who said he had no intention of following what Mr. MacInnis had said, as he had heard these pacifist speeches in the House before!

On May 12, 1939, after the war was over, the question was raised of a grant of $10,000 to an international commission sponsored by the League of Nations for the assistance of child refugees in Spain. Mr. Landeryou questioned the validity of this grant, as there were child refugees in Hull in need of relief. The question came up again under supply (fisheries) on May 31st, and Mr. Michaud explained that the money was being used to cover the cost of a shipment of fish to refugee children in Spain:

The government of Canada thought it advisable to send dried fish to Spain because in years past Spain was a very good customer of Canada for dried fish, and we thought we should renew our good relations.[7]

After some questioning, he admitted that the fish went to children under the control of the Franco regime, not to the refugee children in France, who were, of course, not a potential market.

Except for a few brief questions on the Spanish situation, this account represents the sum total of Canada's involvement in the Spanish Civil War as seen in the House of Commons. It is precisely what could be expected from previous sources: a futile defence of the elected Spanish government by the CCF on the grounds of international law, encountering a blank wall of government and House disinterest, nervousness about Canadian involvement and absolute reliance on British policy, in this case exactly what Mr. King desired.

CHAPTER 7

Conclusion

The Canadian volunteers initially served in the Lincoln and Washington Battalions, and many members of the Mackenzie-Papineau Battalion were Americans. It is therefore interesting to compare Allen Guttmann's general conclusions on American sentiment to my findings on the reaction to the Civil War in Canada.

Guttmann describes the passionate concern for the Loyalist cause felt by many Americans as "one more manifestation of the Liberal tradition in America."[1] Surveys have shown that a large group of American Roman Catholics supported the Loyalists. Guttmann also believed that the conservative and Protestant publications were tempted to support Franco as he was fighting against the "New Deal" and "Communism," but that a commitment to liberal democracy or a dislike of Roman Catholicism kept them from it. In Canada, the hostility of the Roman Catholic Church towards the Spanish government was very evident. I did not examine Protestant church papers except for the United Church publication, *New Outlook*, between July and December 1936. During this period it carried only one pro-Loyalist editorial and several pacifist ones.

Despite American liberal and radical sympathy for the Republic, American foreign policy was definite in its obstruction of the Republican cause. The reasons given in *The Wound in the Heart* are as follows: American foreign policy was greatly influenced by the British policy of non-intervention; most Americans were anxious to avoid involvement in "European wars"; the Catholic Church hierarchy was determined to block any move to help the Republicans. All these reasons applied to Canada as well, but not to the same extent for French- and English-speaking Canadians. The French-language newspapers showed no concern with British policy, and English-language publications only emphasized the first two arguments. However, Canadian publications shared an intense fear of Communism, evidently stronger than that found in the American press at the time. Some Conservative papers supported the policy of neutrality on the strength of a Communist takeover before it had ever occurred, thus ensuring eventual Communist control of the Loyalist government.

According to Guttmann, many Americans felt that Loyalist Spain exemplified the spirit of 1776 and the ideals of liberty, equality and fraternity, and they identified with a subject class throwing off its oppressors and taking over the land, the factories and the peace-keeping. In contrast, Professor Frank Underhill has stated that Canada does not possess the revolutionary tradition found in the United States.[2] Certainly revolutions did not appeal to publications proud of a background of British parliamentary tradition and a frontier protected by the Royal Canadian Mounted Police from the kind of lawlessness that occurred in the American west. Professor Robert McDougall has written that the Americans took over the only myths appropriate to the continent, the Adamite myth and the ideology of democratic egalitarianism.[3] These differences may help to explain why support for the Loyalists was found in many popular publications in the United States, while in Canada support was usually confined to small radical ones.

PROGRESS!

Toronto Star, January 31, 1939. Metropolitan Toronto Library Board photo.

THE STAR'S GREG CLARK BENDS AN EAR TO THE O.C.

While the troop train carrying 270 men of the Mackenzie-Papineau battalion of the International brigade sped from Halifax, Major Edward Cecil-Smith of Toronto (RIGHT) related to Gregory Clark of The Star (LEFT) exploits of his comrades in the Spanish civil war. Major Cecil-Smith commanded the group of Canadians during their active service.

Toronto Star, February 6, 1939. Metropolitan Toronto Library Board photo.

Given Guttmann's analysis, one might expect to find more volunteers for Spain from the United States. However, according to Professor Victor Hoar, no country except France sent so large a number of volunteers in proportion to her population as did Canada, more than 1,200 from a population of 12 million.[4] He stated that the large number of volunteers reflected an emotional involvement and identification with the Spanish people due to the alienation of the working class from the previous Conservative government.

Another factor in Canadian participation was that ethnic polarization of volunteers was more possible in Canada than in the United States. Professor Hoar recognized three main groups of volunteers: Anglo-Saxons from British Columbia, Ukrainians from the Prairies, and Finns from Ontario. The last two groups had inherited European radical views and had maintained this tradition in newspapers in their own languages. We have

Walter Hellund and Alex Forbes on their way home from Spain, February 1939. National Archives of Canada/C-67449.

seen the empathy of the *Winnipeg Free Press* with the Loyalist cause and its relation to the European background of its readers.

Volunteers from British Columbia exemplified the radical labour sentiment so strong in that province. According to Professor Hoar, one out of every four men who marched to Regina in 1935 served in Spain as a volunteer. The fact that the Communist Party of Canada worked in the relief camps for single men throughout the Depression helped it to recruit volunteers for the Mackenzie-Papineau Battalion. Moreover, British Columbia's warm climate offered a haven for the unemployed, which might be yet another reason for the many volunteers from that area.

The median age for Canadian volunteers was 32, compared to 26 for Americans, so the Canadians were men whose loyalties had been built up over years of the Depression. While the CCF did not produce as many volunteers as the Communist Party did, it had an important influence on public opinion. In spite of Guttmann's emphasis on the liberal tradition of the United States, the influence of the American Socialist Party was minimal compared to that of the CCF. Geographically, Canada is larger than the United States, but her relatively small population concentrated over a smaller area meant fewer diverse loyalties, and Loyalist support was able to polarize along ethnic and ideological lines already in existence.

Perhaps the strong support for Franco that existed in some parts of Canada helped the Loyalist cause as well. Several groups saw Fascism as an abuse of civil rights: the working class radicals, the militant left wing and those who had no particular ideological axe to grind, who saw in Spain a threat

Friends-of-Franco Society Celebrates

Winnipeg Free Press, February 25, 1939, National Archives of Canada.

to world peace.

The men who volunteered to fight in Spain went in the face of government opposition, and it appears that few returned disillusioned about the Loyalists or their cause. For some, that came later; others always remembered it as a crusade.

Gerald Brenan has said of the Spanish Civil War that it appeared as if "the fortunes of the civilized world were being played out in miniature, but the actuality was different."[5] Brenan asserts that at the beginning of the war, two sides were clearly drawn, but the alliance of the Roman Catholic provinces with the left and the differences in the aims of the Anarchists and Socialists clouded the issue. He says that outside interference tipped the scales, leaving only the Fascist Falange and the Communists as combattants.

The confusion of loyalties in Spain was reflected in the number of people in other countries who could not decide where they stood. Surveys showed this figure to have been between 24 and 30 percent in the United States, and the men I interviewed for

this study estimated the proportion of disinterested and undecided in Canada to have been at least that large. Aside from the disinterested Canadians, a large group of French- and English-speaking Canadians were willing to accept Franco in order to avoid Communism, and these seemed to constitute a larger percentage of the total population than in the United States, although this is a very difficult figure to determine in a survey of this type. Opposed to this group were the Loyalist supporters, proportionately fewer than their American counterparts, but with strong ethnic and labour backgrounds and organization. Supported by some popular newspapers and by radical publications, they were perhaps better able to accept Communism as part of the struggle against Fascism. It is unusual for Canadians to hold such widespread reactions to a war in Europe. Perhaps this diversity was caused by the complex nature of Spain itself. As Pierre van Paassen mentioned, there was a curious decentralizing tendency in the Spanish people, who detested all forms of government. Such an attitude may have contri-

CANADA TO ADM
FRANCO'S TRIUI

By R. W. LIPSETT

Ottawa, Feb. 28.—The stage is set for Canadian recognition of General Franco's government in Spain.

Officials stressed that there is no reason for haste and neither is there any cause for delay. It has been agreed that after Britain's recognition Canadian action would be a pure formality. It may take place this week. The matter does not require any action by parliament, advice from the department of external affairs that Franco's government is recognized being all required. The subject may find its way into the House, however.

Toronto Star, February 28, 1939. Metropolitan Toronto Library Board photo.

buted its own ferocity to the bitterness particular to Civil Wars.

In the interview quoted at the beginning of this study André Malraux said he "attached a very great importance to the Spanish Civil War not only as a struggle but also because it was a most profound experience of brotherhood." That sentiment is perhaps the reason why so many authors look back nostalgically to those days, or regret not participating in the war. Most volunteers came from either the intelligentsia or the working class, their *esprit de corps* from their belief that their cause was just and for all men and women.

In Canada, many of those who stayed behind failed until too late to accept Loyalist Spain as a legal government fighting the menace of Fascism in Europe. Their belated realization of the significance of what happened in Spain may have caused the peculiar mixture of guilt and pride the sight of the returning veterans inspired. Journalist Greg Clarke,

who met the survivors of the Mac-Paps in Halifax in 1939 and travelled with them to Toronto, wrote: "I don't recollect ever seeing soldiers who inspired in me so strange a mixture of reverence and humiliation and embarrassment at meeting their gaze."[6] Matthew Halton, foreign correspondent for the *Toronto Star*, travelled with the Canadian volunteers from Newhaven, England to their port of embarkation. He described the lasting feeling of brotherhood and support for the Spanish government the volunteers maintained to the very end of the war.

The men were told that a small gift of money from the Spanish government would be awaiting them at Liverpool. At this a wounded man raised his head and said: "Spain owes us nothing! There's nothing coming to us!" And he added later: "No matter what happens to me for the rest of my life, there's one thing nothing can ever take away; I fought for the Spanish people."[7]

NOTES

Introduction

[1]Philip Toynbee, *Friends Apart,* quoted in *Journey to the Frontier – Julian Bell and John Cornford: their lives and the 1930s,* by P. Stanky and W. Abrahams (London: Constable, 1966), p. 18.

[2]*Telegraph Journal*, Saint John, N.B., October 20, 1986.

[3]Editorial, *Ottawa Citizen*, February 1, 1988.

CHAPTER 1
"The Darkling Plain"

[1]Allen Guttmann used this quotation from Albert Camus as the source of his title, *The Wound in the Heart*. He did not give its location and I have been unable to trace it.

[2]"André Malraux on Man's Value," by Henry Tanner of the *New York Times*, reprinted in the *Ottawa Journal*, November 2, 1968.

[3]Vincent Brome, *The International Brigades: Spain 1936-39* (London: Wm. Heinemann Ltd., 1965), p. 3.

[4]Hugh Thomas, *The Spanish Civil War*, rev. ed. (London: Penguin Books, 1965), p. 231.

[5]Thomas, p. 356.

[6]Victor Hoar, *The Mackenzie-Papineau Battalion: Canadian Participation in the Spanish Civil War* (Toronto: Copp Clark, 1969), p. 8.

[7]Correspondence, *New Frontier*, December 1936, p. 16.

CHAPTER 2
"The Church's one foundation is now the Moslem sword"

[1]Louis A. MacKay, "Battle Hymn for the Spanish Rebels," *Canadian Forum*, September 1936.

[2]All the circulation figures and descriptive titles given for newspapers are taken from *McKim's Directory of Canadian Publications* for 1937, which lists circulation figures for the previous year.

[3]Carlton McNaught, *Canada Gets the News* (Toronto: Ryerson Press, 1940).

[4]Warren Breed, "Social Control in the Newsroom: A Functional Analysis," *Social Forces* 33, no. 4 (May 1955), pp. 326-35.

[5]Leo C. Rosten, *The Washington Correspondents* (New York: Harcourt & Brace, 1937).

[6]"Trouble in Spain," editorial, *Montreal Gazette,* July 21, 1936.

[7]"Spanish Leader Issues Warning," editorial, *Montreal Gazette,* August 31, 1936.

[8]"Communism a New Danger," editorial, Toronto *Globe,* July 15, 1936.

[9]"Spain Faces Change," editorial, Toronto *Globe,* July 23, 1936.

[10]"Spain's New Danger," editorial, Toronto *Globe,* August 1, 1936.

[11]"Meddling in Spain's Revolt," editorial, Toronto *Globe,* August 5, 1936.

[12]"Britain's Hands Tied," editorial, Toronto *Globe,* August 6, 1936.

[13]*La Patrie,* August 13, 1936.

[14]*Ibid.,* July 27, 1936.

[15]*Le Devoir,* July 27, 1936.

[16]*Ibid.,* August 29, 1936.

[17]*La Patrie,* August 22, 1936.

[18]Ross Harkness, *J.E. Atkinson of The Star* (Toronto: University of Toronto Press, 1963), p. 304.

[19]Allen Guttmann, *The Wound in the Heart: America and the Spanish Civil War* (New York: Free Press of Glencoe, 1962), p. 29.

[20]"More German Unity," editorial, *Montreal Gazette,* November 9, 1936.

[21]"Britain's Policy Towards Spain," editorial, *Montreal Gazette,* November 25, 1936.

[22]*Montreal Gazette,* December 1, 1936.

[23]"The Government and Communism," editorial, *Montreal Gazette,* December 21, 1936.

[24]"Mr. Eden's Christmas Cheer," editorial, *Montreal Gazette,* December 21, 1936.

[25]"U.S. Neutrality Law a Misnomer," editorial, *Montreal Gazette,* December 30, 1936.

[26]"A Diplomatic Steal," editorial, *Globe and Mail,* November 19, 1936.

[27]"Britain the Diplomatic Goat," editorial, *Globe and Mail,* November 10, 1936.

[28]"Empire's Internal Danger," editorial, *Globe and Mail,* November 30, 1936.

[29]"Opposition No Defense," *Globe and Mail,* December 18, 1936.

[30]James Eayrs, "A Low Dishonest Decade: Aspects of Canadian External Policy, 1931-39," in *The Growth of Canadian Policies in External Affairs,* ed. Hugh L. Keenleyside et al. (Durham, N.C., 1960), pp. 68-9.

[31]"Spain Remains Dangerous," editorial, *Globe and Mail,* December 21, 1936.

[32]"What Next, Hitler?" editorial, *Globe and Mail,* December 25, 1936.

[33]"Les Origines de la Guerre Civile en Espagne," *Le Devoir,* October 31, 1936.

[34]"La Résistance de Madrid," *Le Devoir,* November 11, 1936.

[35]"L'Espagne et le Communisme," *Le Devoir,* November 16, 1936.

[36]*Le Devoir,* November 30, 1936.

[37]*Ibid.,* December 22, 1936.

[38]*La Patrie,* November 6, 1936.

[39]*Ibid.,* November 16, 1936.

[40]"Méditation en Espagne," editorial, *La Patrie,* December 30, 1936.

[41]Thomas, p. 539.

[42]"Misunderstanding Spanish Events," editorial, *Globe and Mail,* May 5, 1937.

[43]"Murder from Air in Spanish War," *Globe and Mail,* May 27, 1937.

[44]*La Patrie*, April 27, 1937.

[45]*Ibid.*, April 30, 1937.

[46]"Propagande Revolutionaire," *Le Droit*, May 1, 1937.

[47]*Montreal Gazette*, February 2, 1939.

[48]*Ibid.*

[49]"The Spanish War Continues," editorial, *Montreal Gazette*, February 7, 1939.

[50]"The Debris of War in Spain," editorial, *Montreal Gazette*, February 17, 1939.

[51]"Freedom's Only Chance," editorial, *Globe and Mail*, January 25, 1939.

[52]"Further Struggle Futile," editorial, *Globe and Mail*, January 31, 1939.

[53]*Globe and Mail*, February 22, 1939.

[54]*Le Devoir*, February 28, 1939.

[55]"La Chute de Barcelone et Les Legendes," editorial, *La Patrie*, January 27, 1939.

[56]"Coups d'oeil sur la guerre civile d'Espagne," *La Patrie*, February 12, 1939.

[57]*Globe and Mail*, December 2, 1937.

[58]George V. Ferguson, "Freedom of the Press," in *Press and Party in Canada: Issues of Freedom*, ed. G. Ferguson and F. Underhill (Toronto: Ryerson Press, 1955), p. 4.

CHAPTER 3

"Spain is a scar on my heart"

[1]Extract from a letter written by Dr. Norman Bethune to his wife from Hong Kong in 1938, quoted in *The Scalpel, The Sword*, by Ted Allan and Sydney Gordon (1952: reprint, Toronto: McClelland and Stewart, 1976), p. 167.

[2]Wilfred H. Kesterton, *A History of Journalism in Canada*, Carleton Library Series, no. 36 (Toronto: McClelland and Stewart, 1967), p. 97.

[3]"Events in Spain," editorial, *Winnipeg Free Press*, July 24, 1936.

[4]"Spain and Europe," editorial, *Winnipeg Free Press*, August 8, 1936.

[5]"Outlook in Europe," editorial, *Winnipeg Free Press*, August 28, 1936.

[6]*Montreal Gazette*, October 24, 1936.

[7]J. King Gordon, "Fascist Weekend in Montreal," *Christian Century*, November 25, 1936, pp. 1560-62.

[8]"Dear Old Liberty," *Saturday Night*, November 14, 1936.

[9]G(eorge) V. F(erguson), "Quebec Fascism," *Winnipeg Free Press*, November 3, 1936.

[10]*Vancouver Province*, November 9, 1936.

[11]"Events in Spain," editorial, *Winnipeg Free Press*, November 9, 1936.

[12]Thomas, p. 386.

[13]"None So Blind," editorial, *Winnipeg Free Press*, December 19, 1936.

[14]*Winnipeg Free Press*, February 7, 1939.

[15]"General Franco's Triumph," editorial, *Winnipeg Free Press*, February 28, 1939.

[16]"The Civil War in Spain," editorial, *Toronto Star*, July 21, 1936.

[17]"The War in Spain," editorial, *Toronto Star*, August 20, 1936.

[18]"France's Temptation," editorial, *Toronto Star*, August 28, 1936.

[19]"Time on Madrid's Side," editorial, *Toronto Star*, August 29, 1936.

[20]Voice of the People, *Toronto Star*, August 31, 1936.

[21]Thomas, p. 402.

[22]Voice of the People, *Toronto Star*, November 7, 1936.

[23]*Toronto Star*, November 12, 1936.

[24]"Recognition of the Rebels," editorial, *Toronto Star*, November 19, 1936.

[25]*Toronto Star*, December 12, 1936.

[26]*Ibid.*

[27]"Spain Grows Dangerous," editorial, *Toronto Star*, December 21, 1936.

[28]*Toronto Star*, December 24, 1936.

[29]Voice of the People, *Toronto Star*, February 2, 1939.

[30]*Toronto Star*, February 3, 1939.

[31]*Ibid.*, February 4, 1939.

[32]"Winding up the Civil War," editorial, *Toronto Star*, February 10, 1939.

[33]*Toronto Star*, February 11, 1939.

[34]*Ibid.*, February 27, 1939.

[35]*Ibid.*, February 28, 1939.

CHAPTER 4

Periodicals Pro and Con

[1]London Letter, *Maclean's*, September 1, 1936.

[2]"Do You Want It Here?" editorial, *Maclean's*, December 1, 1936.

[3]London Letter – "The War in Spain," *Maclean's*, March 1, 1937.

[4]London Letter – "Britain's Gamble for Peace," *Maclean's*, January 15, 1938.

[5]London Letter – "My Canadian Critics," *Maclean's*, December 15, 1938.

[6]"Opinions of the Weak," editorial, *Saturday Night*, August 29, 1936.

[7]"Canada's World View," editorial, *Saturday Night*, August 29, 1936.

[8]"Keeping Out of Spain," editorial, *Saturday Night*, October 3, 1936.

[9]"Too Lofty a Code," editorial, *Saturday Night*, October 3, 1936.

[10]Jean Houpert, "First Days of Civil War in the Spanish Capital," *Saturday Night*, October 24, 1936.

[11]Hugh Shoobridge, "Wings Over Everywhere," *Saturday Night*, May 1, 1937.

[12]"Not Quite Fair to Spain," editorial, *Saturday Night*, January 14, 1939.

[13]*Saturday Night*, February 11, 1939.

[14]"The Soldiers' Return," editorial, *Saturday Night*, February 11, 1939.

[15]"The Front Page," editorial, *Saturday Night*, March 4, 1939.

[16]"Without Precedent," editorial, *New Commonwealth*, September 5, 1936.

[17]"To Offer Field Hospital," *New Commonwealth*, September 26, 1936.

[18]Tim Buck, "Soldiers of democracy," *Marxist Quarterly* 18 (Summer, 1966).

[19]Thomas, p. 771.

[20]*Montreal Gazette*, June 18, 1937.

[21]"Vancouver Volunteers Off to Spain," *Federationist*, February 18, 1937.

[22]*Federationist*, April 29, 1937.

[23]*Ibid.*, May 29, 1937.

[24]*Ibid.*, August 12, 1937.

25*Ibid.*, March 17, 1938.

26*Ibid.*, August 4, 1938.

27"Plan Welcome for Spanish War Vets," *Federationist*, February 9, 1939.

28"Spain," editorial, *Canadian Forum*, September 1936.

29"Spain," editorial, *Canadian Forum*, October 1936.

30"Non-Intervention Making Gesture," editorial, *Canadian Forum*, September 1937.

31"Civil War in Spain," editorial, *New Frontier*, September 1936.

32"The International Scene," editorial, *New Frontier*, November 1936.

33"Where I stand on Spain," *New Frontier*, December 1936.

34"The New Commonwealth and the Election," editorial, *New Frontier*, January 1937.

35*New Frontier*, May 1937.

36*Ibid.*, April 1936.

CHAPTER 5
"The Crystal Spirit"

1*Canadian Forum*, April 1939.

2L.A. MacKay, "Murder Most Foul," *Canadian Forum*, December 1937.

3Dorothy Livesay, "Spain," *New Frontier*, June 1937.

4Lionel Reid, "Salutes," *Canadian Forum*, August 1938.

5William Robbins, "To L-- B--," *Canadian Forum*, September 1938.

6David Andrade, "Dust Patterns after the Revolution," *Canadian Forum*, March 1939.

7A.M. Klein, "Sonnet without Music," *Canadian Forum*, June 1938.

8F.W. Watt, "Literature of Protest," in *Literary History of Canada*, ed. Carl Klinck (Toronto: University of Toronto Press, 1965), p. 473.

9Ted Allan, *This Time a Better Earth* (New York: Wm. Morrow, 1939), p. 218.

10Hugh MacLennan, *The Watch That Ends the Night* (Toronto: Macmillan, 1958), p. 4.

11*Ibid.*, p. 100.

12*Ibid.*, p. 244.

13*Ibid.*, p. 323.

14Gerald Brenan, *The Spanish Labyrinth: An Account of the Social and Political Background of the Civil War* (Cambridge: Cambridge University Press, 1943), p. xv.

CHAPTER 6
Vox Populi

1Canada, House of Commons *Debates*, Session 1937, Vol. 1, pp. 64-65.

2*Ibid.*, Vol. 2, p. 1944.

3*Ibid.*, p. 1951-52.

4*Ibid.*, p. 1958.

5*Ibid.*, Session 1938, Vol. 2, p. 1407.

6*Ibid.*, Vol. 3, p. 3186-87.

7*Ibid.*, Session 1939, Vol. 14, p. 4814.

CHAPTER 7
Conclusion

1Guttmann, p. 3.

2Frank H. Underhill, "Some Reflections on the Liberal Tradition in Canada," in *Approaches to Canadian History*, ed. William Mackintosh et al. (Toronto: University of Toronto Press, 1967), p. 36.

3Robert McDougall, "The Dodo and the Cruising Auk: Class in Canadian Literature," *Canadian Literature*, no. 18 (Autumn 1963), p. 9.

4Victor Hoar, "Canadians in the Spanish Civil War: The Way Over," *Dalhousie Review* 48, no. 1 (Spring 1968), p. 101.

5Brenan, p. xv.

6*Toronto Star*, February 1939, quoted in Hugh Garner, review of *The Mackenzie-Papineau Battalion* by Victor Hoar, *Globe and Mail*, April 5, 1969.

7Matthew Halton, *Ten Years to Alamein* (Toronto: S.J. Reginald Saunders, 1944), p. 35.

BIBLIOGRAPHY

Government Documents

Canada. House of Commons *Debates,* 1937-39.

Newspapers

Le Devoir.
Le Droit.
Globe and Mail.
Regina Leader-Post.
Montreal Gazette.
La Patrie.
Toronto Star.
Vancouver Province.
Winnipeg Free Press.

Periodicals

Canadian Forum.
The Federationist.
Maclean's.
Marxist Quarterly 18 (Summer 1966).
New Commonwealth.
New Frontier.
Saturday Night.

Books

Allan, Ted [Alan Herman, pseud.]. *This Time a Better Earth.* New York: Wm. Morrow, 1939.

Allan, Ted and Sydney Gordon. *The Scalpel, The Sword: The Story of Dr. Norman Bethune.* 1952. Reprint. Toronto: McClelland and Stewart, 1976.

Birney, Earle. *Down the Long Table.* Toronto: McClelland and Stewart, 1955.

Bolloten, Burnett. *The Grand Camouflage: The Communist Conspiracy in the Spanish Civil War.* London: Hollis & Carter, 1961.

Brenan, Gerald. *The Spanish Labyrinth: An Account of the Social and Political Background of the Civil War.* Cambridge: Cambridge University Press, 1943.

Brome, Vincent. *The International Brigades: Spain 1936-39.* London: Wm. Heinemann, 1965.

de Palencia, Isabel. *Smouldering Freedom: The Story of the Spanish Republicans in Exile.* Toronto: Longmans, Green, 1945.

Guttmann, Allen. *The Wound in the Heart: America and the Spanish Civil War.* New York: Free Press of Glencoe, 1962.

Halton, Matthew. *Ten Years to Alamein.* Toronto: S.J. Reginald Saunders, 1944.

Harkness, Ross. *J.E. Atkinson of The Star.* Toronto: University of Toronto Press, 1963.

Hoar, Victor. *The Mackenzie-Papineau Battalion: Canadian Participation in the Spanish Civil War.* Toronto: Copp Clark, 1969.

Horn, Michiel. *Years of Despair, 1929-39.* Toronto: Grolier, 1986.

Kesterton, Wilfred. *A History of Journalism in Canada.* Carleton Library Series, no. 36. Toronto: McClelland and Stewart, 1967.

Koestler, Arthur. "Dialogue with Death." In *Spanish Testament.* London: Victor Gollancz, 1937.

MacLennan, Hugh. *The Watch That Ends the Night.* Toronto: MacMillan, 1958.

McKim's Directory of Canadian Publications. 1937. Montreal: A. McKim.

McNaught, Carlton. *Canada Gets the News.* Toronto: Ryerson Press, 1940.

Orwell, George. *Homage to Catalonia.* London: Secker & Warburg, 1938.

Pritchett, Victor. *The Spanish Temper.* New York: Alfred A. Knopf, 1954.

Puzzo, Dante A. *Spain and the Great Powers 1936-1941.* New York: Columbia University Press, 1962.

Rosten, Leo. *The Washington Correspondents.* New York: Harcourt & Brace, 1937.

Ruiz Vilaplana, Antonio. *Burgos Justice. A Year's Experience of Nationalist Spain.* London: Constable, 1938.

Steeves, Dorothy. *The Compassionate Rebel: Ernest E. Winch and His Times.* Vancouver: Boag Foundation, 1960.

Thomas, Hugh. *The Spanish Civil War.* Rev. ed. London: Penguin Books, 1965.

Weintraub, Stanley. *The Last Great Cause: The Intellectuals and the Spanish Civil War.* New York: Weybright & Talley, 1968.

Woodcock, George. *Anarchism: A History of Libertarian Movements.* New York: The World Publishing, 1962.

————. *The Crystal Spirit: A Study of George Orwell.* London: Jonathan Cape, 1966.

Wyden, Peter. *The Passionate War: The Narrative History of the Spanish Civil War, 1936-39.* New York: Simon & Schuster, 1983.

Articles

Breed Warren. "Social Control in the Newsroom: A Functional Analysis." *Social Forces* 33, no. 4 (May 1955): pp. 326-35.

Careless, J.M.S. "Limited Identities in Canada." *Canadian Historical Review* L, no. 1 (March 1969): pp. 1-10.

Ferguson, George. "Freedom of the Press." In *Press and Party in Canada: Issues of Freedom,* edited by G. Ferguson and F. Underhill, pp. 1-23. Toronto: Ryerson Press, 1955.

Gordon, J. King. "Fascist Weekend in Montreal." *Christian Century* LIII (November 25, 1936), pp. 1560-62.

Hoar, Victor. "Canadians in the Spanish Civil War: The Way Over." *Dalhousie Review* 48, no. 1 (Spring 1968), pp. 100-13.

McDougall, Robert. "The Dodo and the Cruising Auk: Class in Canadian Literature." *Canadian Literature,* no. 18 (Autumn 1963), pp. 6-20.

Underhill, Frank. "Some Reflections on the Liberal Tradition in Canada." In *Approaches to Canadian History,* edited by William Mackintosh et al., pp. 29-41. Toronto: University of Toronto Press, 1967.

Watt, F.W. "Literature of Protest." In *Literary History of Canada,* edited by Carl Klinck, pp. 457-73. Toronto: University of Toronto Press, 1965.

Unpublished Material

Fenrick, William. "The Intellectual as Activist: A Study of the *Canadian Forum* in the Middle 1930's." Master's thesis. Institute of Canadian Studies, Carleton University, Ottawa, 1967.

Wright, Ester. "The External Policy of the C.C.F." Master's thesis. Institute of Canadian Studies, Carleton University, Ottawa, 1964.

Yemen, Bruce. "Porter on the Mass Media: A View of Chapter 15 of *The Vertical Mosaic*." Paper for Department of Sociology, Carleton University, Ottawa, 1969.

Interviews

Dr. Eugene Forsey. Interview with author. November 1968.
Mr. Wilfred Kesterton. Interview with author. April 1969.
Professor Frank Scott. Interview with author. February 1969.
Mr. Hazen Sise. Interview with author. March 1969.
Mr. Graham Spry. Interview with author. January 1969.
Mr. Justice Thorson. Interview with author. January 1969.

INDEX